## PRAISE FOR
# IF MY HEART HAD WINGS

"Loved it! The Greatest Generation all have their secrets in this endlessly fascinating & compelling memoir." – *Reedsy Discovery*

"A unique book, written about real people and events... one of the best in the WWII genre!" – *Amazon Reader*

"Not the usual WWII story, *If My Heart Had Wings* is at once poignant and heartbreaking. Well written and edited, it was a joy to read."– *Marion Marchetto, author of Bridgewater Chronicles*

"Superb! A wonderful story of devotion and tough times... I thoroughly enjoyed it!" – *C. Paul Hilliard, Vice Chairman, Board of Trustees, National WWII Museum*

"[Taylor has] mastered a conversational yet detail resonant style of prose. I know I can hear my mother and grandmother in her writing, musing and conversing." – *Misanthropester.com*

"The book is subtitled "A World War II Love Story," but it is so much more than that. I recommend it to anyone who likes World War II tales and stories about strong women who never give in to adversity." – *Miss Dorothy, Vine Voice*

A deeply moving tribute, meticulously researched and engaging from start to finish." – *Carol Starr Schneider, author of Brushes: A Comedy of Hairs*

# If My Heart Had Wings

## *A World War II Love Story*

NADINE TAYLOR

ISBN: 9780692057803

*For Mom, with all my love*

# CONTENTS

# FOREWORD

World War II saw more than 80 million men in uniform engaged in battle on every continent and every ocean around the world. Out of this greatest of all conflicts came millions of stories of love and loss, including this one—special because it's not only about a lost soldier, but also about those left behind who must deal with that loss forever.

*If My Heart Had Wings* is a tale well-told; a beautiful narrative reminding us that when we lose someone we love, we pay with grief. And the greater the love, the greater the grief.

But would we have it any other way?

*C. Paul Hilliard, Vice Chairman, Board of Trustees*
*The National World War II Museum*

## Prologue

Their wedding picture was so typical of the World War II years. Mom was dressed to the nines in a chic pearl grey suit with padded shoulders and a pencil-slim skirt, set off by a little pink hat perched toward the front of her head and surrounded by puffs of pink tulle. Dad was every inch the perfect groom in a black double-breasted suit with a jaunty white carnation on his lapel.

My sister Dawn and I often lingered over this picture of our parents as we flipped through their wedding album, if you could call it an album. It was more like a spiral-bound notebook holding about a dozen 8 x 10 black and white pictures in plastic sheet protectors. They didn't need anything fancy, Mom said, so they settled on the cheapest package available. Still, Dawn and I agreed that the photographer should have gotten at least one shot of Mom walking down the aisle with her eyes open. In the only picture that survives, she approaches her new life with her eyelids firmly shut.

"There goes Mom," we liked to say, "sleepwalking down the aisle!"

Nineteen forty-six was a big year for weddings, when soldiers came home from World War II eager to reunite with their sweethearts, get married, start families, and get on with the business of living. My parents were no different, although they didn't know each other very well when they tied the knot in March of that year. They had met briefly during the war and corresponded for two years. Then, when Dad got back to the

States, they spent two months getting to know each other and trying to decide if they had something that could last.

When the answer turned out to be yes, Mom booked a church and headed downtown in search of an attractive yet practical suit. There was no point in spending money on some silly dress you could only wear once, she told us, when you could buy a high-quality suit for the same price (or less) and wear it over and over again. Which is exactly what she did. That pearl grey suit became one of her wardrobe staples. In fact, she was able to wear it to work until she was seven months pregnant with my sister.

So you can imagine my surprise when, at the age of thirteen, I was out in the garage, riffling through a drawer full of black and white photos, when I came upon a picture of my mother in a white wedding gown, complete with a shoulder-length veil! It was the summer of 1966; my sister was seventeen, my parents had been married for twenty years, and as far as I knew, there had never been any mention of a white wedding dress.

I hightailed it down the driveway and burst through the kitchen door, waving the picture. Mom was standing at the stove stirring something, while Dawn was busy chopping tomatoes at the kitchen counter.

"Mom!" I shouted, thrusting the picture at her. "I thought you got married in a *suit!*"

She looked at the picture, smiled sheepishly, and said slowly, "Well, I guess I always knew I was going to have to tell you girls someday... I was married before."

My sister and I looked at each other with jaws dropped. There had never been the slightest mention of *any* romantic relationship in Mom's past, much less a *husband*! Dumbfounded, we looked at our mother with eyes that demanded an explanation.

"It happened during the war, before I knew your father," she said, trying to brush it off like an unwanted piece of lint.

"Well, who was he?" I demanded.

"He was my college boyfriend."

"Did you have any kids?" I asked, panicked, imagining some strange family member suddenly materializing on our front porch.

"No," she smiled, trying to calm me down. "There were no kids. And anyway, it all happened a long time ago. It doesn't matter anymore."

With that, she turned back to her stirring; discussion ended.

I was so shocked by her news that I couldn't think of anything else to say. So I scurried back to the garage to see if I could find any other interesting (and possibly stunning) pictures. I couldn't.

There was a time, when I was very young, when I couldn't imagine that my mother had had a life before I existed. Once I got a little older, I realized that she'd married my father and given birth to my sister before I was born, so I began to think of her life as starting once she met Dad. But I also knew that she had been a child once, just like me; I'd seen the pictures. So I revised my idea

3

once again and thought of her life as a two-part affair: her childhood and Dad/us.

But once I found the white wedding picture, it became glaringly apparent that at least one other part of her life had existed, the part involving another man and another marriage. It was such a bizarre notion that I simply blocked it at first. But the older I got, the more curious I became about this secret life of hers. It seemed so mysterious and romantic—two adjectives I normally wouldn't have applied to my pragmatic, matter-of-fact mother. And the more I looked into it, the more obsessed I became.

This is the story of what my mother was like before she had me. It's also the story of secrets, lies, a love that never died, and a woman's long journey to self-discovery and fulfillment. It would take me decades to uncover these secrets, using letters, an Army personnel file, interviews with family members, and, of course, the many stories, vignettes, and insights that Mom relayed to me over the years. And in the process, not only did I learn the true story of my mother, but I also discovered the story of myself.

**The white wedding dress – October 27, 1942**

## CHAPTER ONE

# Beginnings

Many years after my discovery of the wedding picture, when my sister and I were well into middle age and trying to come up with ideas for Mom's eulogy, Dawn got on my nerves when she kept referring to Mom as a "farm girl." Mom had left the farm when she was two years old, for crying out loud, and had lived in big cities for the rest of her life. If anything, she was a "city girl."

But I knew what Dawn meant. Mom did come from farm stock and, as such, had a farmer's outlook and approach to life. You know—work hard and take good care of what you've got; you may not be able to replace it. Don't waste anything; there's always another use for it. Stand on your own two feet; don't expect others to come to your rescue. Save as much money as you can; rainy days are sure to come. Even at the end of her life, when she had plenty of money, she was endlessly thrifty and practical. But just about anyone could have predicted this simply by looking at her family history.

My mother, Nina Blanch Ostrom, (Nina rhymes with Dinah), was born in southern Minnesota in 1921 to a pair of hardworking farmers who wanted nothing more than to escape to the big city. My grandfather, Lloyd Ostrom, the eldest son in a family that included seven girls, had inherited the 160-acre farm carved out of the wilderness in the 1860s by his great-grandfather. Unfortunately, even though he'd been raised to this purpose since toddlerhood, Grandpa hated just about everything about farming: the endless work, the long, sweaty days in the field, the crushing responsibility, and the fact that he never knew how much money he would earn until harvest time. If the crop turned out to be poor because of a drought, a plague of locusts, or some other unforeseen circumstance, he was sunk. At best, farming was subsistence living; the lucky ones maintained the status quo, but never really got ahead.

My grandmother Blanch, another third-generation farmer, wholeheartedly shared Grandpa's dim views of farm life. And she also had her own reasons for wanting to ditch the farm. A former teacher in a one-room schoolhouse, Grandma's razor-sharp mind and keen attention to detail were much better suited to a research lab than a farmhouse. And while she had no illusions about becoming a scientist or even a lab technician, if she could move to the big city, she would at least be able to join some clubs or go to a concert now and again, which would help satiate her hungry mind. Even more important, the kids would have a shot at getting a better education, increasing the odds that they would one day have professional careers. Farming was definitely not what Grandma envisioned for them.

It would take my grandparents eight long years of working their tails off and searching for an escape before they finally got their chance. In 1923 Grandpa saw a newspaper ad announcing that Armour & Company, a recently-opened meatpacking plant in South St. Paul, was looking for strong young men who weren't afraid of hard work. And it seemed he was exactly the kind of guy they were seeking: strong, full of stamina, and willing to work ten-hour days, six days a week for a weekly paycheck of $18.75. He was used to a workload like that, so that was no problem. And though the pay seems ridiculously low in modern terms, it was enough to support a family of four in those days. So, he applied for the job, deeded the farm back to his father, grabbed Grandma and their two kids—seven-year-old Ted and two-year-old Nina—and took off for South St. Paul. They would never look back.

Of course, working at a meatpacking plant was no picnic. But Grandpa would hang in there for the next forty years, mostly "slingin' hams," as Dad liked to say, although Mom insisted on the more genteel term of "grading hams." Most likely, at least in the early days, Grandpa also took a turn in other departments, perhaps slicing and packaging finished cuts of meat, cleaning the sewers, hoisting slaughtered steers, and the like. He may have even spent some time on the killing floor, the worst place to work in the entire plant, where men used sledgehammers to bash in the heads of cattle, and the floors ran red with rivers of blood. Working at the plant was not for the weak, the faint-hearted, or those who lacked strong stomachs. Fortunately, Grandpa was none of those.

For the next sixteen years, the Ostroms occupied a two-bedroom house on a modest street in South St. Paul. And just like everyone else, they struggled to make ends meet, especially when the Great Depression took hold at the end of the decade. Grandpa took on an extra job washing down trucks after his regular shift, which lengthened his workday to a grueling fourteen hours. And because the family didn't own a car, he walked a mile and a half to and from work, battling all kinds of weather, including Minnesota's famous blizzards. But he never complained. By example he taught his kids to work hard, do whatever was necessary to meet life's challenges, and swallow any complaints they might have had—there was no point in griping. Life wasn't easy, he told them, but there was always a way to keep going.

Grandma worked just as hard as Grandpa, although in different ways. In addition to doing the household chores and taking excellent care of the children, she established her own small business as a seamstress. Working at home, Grandma dressed entire wedding parties, including the bride, bridesmaids, mothers, flower girls, and ring bearers. Mom remembered that, as a small child, she liked to run her hands over the smooth, beautiful silks and satins that were always piled on the dining room table.

The money Grandma made from her sewing business, coupled with her ability to pinch a penny until it screamed, helped ensure that the family was always well-fed, nicely dressed, and free of debt. She taught her children to be responsible, well-organized, practical, and, of course, frugal. And she passed on her love of anything that engaged the mind: reading, writing, history, arithmetic, games, puzzles, and diagramming sentences.

Ted, who had inherited his mother's sharp mind and was way ahead of the rest of his class, graduated from high school at age sixteen. Nina didn't skip any grades, but she was also bright, with an affinity for both words and numbers. Her well-developed imagination made her popular with the neighborhood kids who liked to loll beneath a tree on hot summer days and listen to the stories she made up. In those days, when everyone was poor and toys were scarce, storytelling skills were in high demand. Her stories had the added advantage of being ongoing. As she would say years later, "Somehow, I always seemed to be able to come up with another chapter, no matter how long the story lasted." It was a gift.

The kids affectionately called Nina "Skinny Bones" because she was thinner than most, even during an era when just about everyone was lean. But by the time she reached high school, "Skinny Bones" had morphed into a slim, curvy brunette with a swan-like neck and the kind of pretty face that needed little makeup. When she wasn't studying, Nina was surrounded by a gaggle of girlfriends and occasionally a few boys. Typical Saturday night fun consisted of squeezing into somebody's old jalopy and heading off to a dance or the movies. Or they might gather around the piano for a singalong, sometimes at the Ostrom's house, where Nina would play. There was no special guy for her during this time, or for most of her girlfriends; just platonic relationships with boys who were fun. And that was enough.

So, in spite of the Depression, life was pretty good for all of the Ostroms. Ted even managed to put himself through college and land a job teaching high school math in northern Minnesota. But just as the Depression was winding down in 1939, the remaining three Ostroms suddenly had a good reason to pull up stakes and leave South St. Paul forever. Nina was graduating from high school in June and wanted to go to college, but there were a few problems. It wasn't that she couldn't handle it. Everyone in the family agreed that she had the necessary brains and the discipline. And Grandma was especially keen on the idea because she saw it as her daughter's ticket to a career, something she herself had been denied. Just as important was the fact that a college campus was the perfect place for Nina to meet a nice, well-educated man to marry. No factory workers or farmers for her.

One problem was money, but that disappeared when Ted generously offered to pay his sister's tuition. The other problem was that all of the universities were located in St. Paul proper, which was ninety minutes away by streetcar, plus walking—a long haul, especially during Minnesota's grueling winters. This alone would probably preclude Nina's participation in any campus activities. So, Grandma and Grandpa decided to bite the bullet and move to St. Paul, where they could all live somewhere close to campus. This, of course, meant that Grandpa would be the one to brave the ninety-minute commute to work. But neither one of my grandparents ever complained about their sacrifices. Setting up their daughter for a successful and happy life took precedence over everything.

Not many women went to college in those days. And even fewer opted for her choice of major: mathematics, which was almost exclusively male territory. But Nina was blessed with a rational, exacting mind and excellent powers of concentration. She'd discovered that esoteric subjects like calculus and math analysis were well within her grasp, and what's more, math as a whole was *fun* for her. All she needed was a set of rules or laws, plus a problem that needed solving, and she was in heaven. Math was a puzzle, one she was quite confident she could solve.

The college of choice (probably Grandma's choice) was Hamline University, the oldest university in St. Paul. It had plenty going for it: Hamline was small (only 690 students in 1939), had an excellent reputation, and was Methodist, the family's religion. This meant Nina would be meeting young men of the "right" faith. What could be more perfect?

She applied to Hamline, was accepted, and just a week after graduating from South St. Paul High, moved with her family to a small house just a few blocks away from the campus.

Two weeks after that, she met her husband-to-be.

Almost three decades later, I fidgeted in front of a full-length mirror, pinned into a half-made dress, while Mom stood behind me with a mouthful of pins, tugging on one of my shoulder seams. It was the summer of 1968, I was fifteen years old, and Mom was in the midst of creating my school wardrobe for fall. Like her own mother, she was an accomplished seamstress who could whip up just about any kind of garment, including prom dresses, tailored jackets, and vinyl raincoats. And she could make them fit perfectly, but *only* after several try-ons and plenty of analysis.

13

Believe me, it could get pretty annoying if you happened to be the one wearing the dress she was endlessly tugging this way and that.

"Now where is that thing coming from?" she mumbled through the pins, frowning and pulling on an unwanted drape that crossed my left shoulder blade. I could see the determination on her face in the mirror.

Oh boy, here we go, I thought. I'll be standing here forever because she's going to figure this out even if it kills her. Bored and antsy, with no hope of relief in sight, I decided to amuse myself by asking a bold question to see how she'd answer it.

"So what was your first husband's name?"

Mom was concentrating so intently it seemed like she barely heard me.

"Hmpf?" she grunted, through the pins.

"You know, your first husband. What was his name?"

She shot me a surprised and annoyed look.

"What brought *that* on?" she asked through lips tightly clamped around the pins.

"I don't know," I said nonchalantly. "Just curious."

She pulled a pin from between her lips and used it to secure a tuck in the fabric, then stood back to survey the effect. Evidently, it looked okay because suddenly all of the pins seemed to have migrated from her mouth to the top of my dresser.

"It was Lyndon," she said distractedly, continuing to analyze her work. "Lyndon Raff." She frowned and tugged again, shaking her head.

"Raff?" I chortled, hoping to keep the conversation going. "Now, there's a weird name! Never heard of *that* one."

She ignored me, picking up another pin and deepening the shoulder seam.

I wasn't going to be put off that easily.

"And did you meet him at a dance, or what?"

She sighed, put in a second pin, and said irritably, "You're pretty darn nosy! Why do you want to know, anyway?"

"I don't know, just curious. You're the one who's always telling me that family history is so important, and I should know my roots."

This was usually a pretty good way to get to her. We come from a long line of family historians who wrote down not only names and dates but actual stories about themselves and their ancestors. As a result, we knew all kinds of stories about our relatives, some of whom dated back as far as the Salem witch trials.

"Well, this has nothing to do with *your* roots," she said airily. "It's part of my life, but not yours."

I couldn't see why she had to be so standoffish. She'd told me all kinds of stuff about people we were barely related to, including her crazy cousin Grace back on the farm who got pregnant by the hired hand. And then Grace's sister went the same way with the same guy. Those people weren't a part of my roots.

Maybe appealing to her vanity would work better.

"Well, I like hearing about your life, especially back in the

15

olden days. What's the difference if it doesn't involve me? It's still you, and I think you're interesting."

She looked at me dubiously, and something between a chuckle and a snort erupted from the back of her throat. That's what she did when she thought something was bunk.

She was right not to be taken in, of course; it wasn't just family history I was after. What I really wanted was to hear everything I could on the subject of romance. In particular, I was searching for answers to questions like: How do people find each other and get together? What do you say to a boy to make him really like you? And what's expected of you after that? It was all a great mystery to me.

And there was another reason I wanted to hear about Mom's hidden romance. I was enormously curious about what she had been like when she was my age. (Well, okay, maybe just a little older.) It was so hard for me to picture my practical, non-romantic, stay-at-home mother in the throes of some passionate love affair. Who was she back then?

I knew, of course, that she had been glamorous; I'd seen the old pictures. In one, she was as dazzling as a movie star, all done up in a fur coat with huge shoulder pads, a black cartwheel hat, and plenty of ruby red lipstick.

She certainly wasn't glamorous now. Not that she was ugly or even un-pretty; she was just plain, an average-looking middle-aged woman with no makeup and short dark hair brushed back from her face.

As for her clothes they were about as far as you could get from fur coats and fancy hats. Around the house, she mostly wore a pair of black shorts and an old tattered white blouse. More than once, she had told me, "You girls and Dad need clothes because you go out into the world. I don't really need many clothes because I just stay at home."

It was true. She and Dad almost never went out. Her life revolved around helping him with his home-based business and using her skills as a seamstress to make whatever the family needed—clothes, drapes, cushion covers, or whatever. She often said that sewing was her creative outlet.

But how did the glamour girl in the fur coat and black cartwheel hat get to this point? *That* girl certainly hadn't spent her life at the sewing machine.

After implanting one final pin into that troublesome shoulder seam, Mom grunted, "Okay, take this thing off and let me get to work on it."

I pulled the dress over my head and handed it over.

"So anyway, are you gonna tell me how you met him?" I asked insistently, pulling on my shorts and top, then flopping expectantly on my fluffy yellow bed.

"Oh, Dene," she said, shaking her head and smiling. "You slay me."

It was one of the corny things she liked to say when she thought I was silly and yet lovable. I think that's what it meant, anyway.

17

Mom settled into a chair, pinned a few skirt sections together, and tossed the pinned-up garment over to me.

"Here. Make yourself useful and baste these seams together."

Then she turned her attention to basting the sleeves into the armholes—a much more intricate task than the one she had just assigned to me.

"Okay," she said resignedly. "What do you want to know?"

Ha! I won.

"Well, how did you meet him?"

"At camp. Church camp."

"*Camp*? How old was he, anyway?"

"Twenty-one."

Twenty-one! In my book camp was for kids or young teenagers, not people who were old enough to drink.

"Bizarre. How old were *you*?"

"Almost eighteen. It wasn't like the camp you've gone to. It was a camp for college kids and young adults. My mother signed me up because we'd just moved to St. Paul, and she thought it would be a good way for me to meet people."

She continued with her stitching.

"Okay, so then what happened? No, wait, let me guess."

I mustered my most romantic voice and cooed, "There you were, sitting around the campfire, when suddenly your eyes met, and you realized this was the one you'd been waiting for ..."

I looked over to see how that was sitting and got her

18

"C'mon now, get serious" look for my efforts.

"Well, was that what it was like?" I asked hopefully.

"No," she said flatly. "Actually, I was smacking some balls around on the tennis court with another girl when these two guys came by and started cheering us on. And pretty soon, we got so self-conscious that we just gave up and started talking to them. One of them was really handsome. And that was Lyndon."

She indicated the sewing that was lying unattended in my lap.

"Hey, how's that basting coming along?"

I made a big show of knotting my thread and taking a tentative stitch or two. I hated basting.

"So, what did you say to him?" I asked, desperate to find out what to say that would make some cute guy like me.

"Oh, I don't know," she said irritably. "Who can remember? We're talking thirty years ago."

I waited to see if she would go on. She did.

"I'm sure it came up that I was new in town and about to start Hamline in the fall. And he probably said he lived right across the street from there. And then I probably said I lived in the same general area."

"Okay. Then what?"

"And then I left."

"You left?"

"Yes."

"But I thought you liked him!"

"I did like him, but I didn't want him to think I was too eager. So I just smiled, picked up my tennis racket, said, 'See you around,' and went back to my cabin."

I didn't get it. Why would she walk away from a cute guy who wanted to talk to her?

"You've got to give these guys enough rope to hang themselves," she explained patiently. "They don't like it if you're too interested."

"Anyway," she continued, "enough of that kind of stuff. Finish that basting, and then you can clean up this room while I get dinner together."

And that was it. Discussion ended.

∞

I never did find out the details of how the two of them connected, other than the tennis game. But I'd gone to camp myself, so I had some idea of how it might have happened.

I could picture them taking a nature hike and getting so wrapped up in talking to each other that they didn't see anything around them.

I could imagine them splashing each other during canoe races and laughing their heads off.

I could see them holding on to each other's waists and falling down during three-legged races.

I could envision them sitting a little too close to each other while they toasted marshmallows on a stick, and doing all the other corny, ridiculously fun things that campers do.

20

And somehow, somewhere, while they were gliding across a lake, or singing in front of a campfire, or just sitting on a tree stump talking about what they wanted to do in the fall, a spark was struck.

And that spark became a flame.

**Mom, about the time she met Lyndon**

I remember the summer of 1968 as being an incredibly long and tedious one. At fifteen, I didn't have a driver's license yet and neither did any of my friends, so tooling around the town was out. I was too young to work and had recently given up my ballet lessons, which left just one activity to occupy my time: six weeks of summer school, during which I took World History and Design Craft—whoopee. I spent the rest of my time reading my boring history book, helping Mom make my fall wardrobe, and pumping her for romantic stories about Lyndon.

I tried to get her going again just a few days after she told me about meeting Lyndon on the tennis court.

We were on our hands and knees on the living room floor, where she was showing me how to cut out my next dress.

"First of all," she instructed solemnly, "Don't ever buy the amount of yardage listed on the pattern; it's a waste of money. You can always get it out in less. Look at this! The pattern calls for two yards and I bought a yard and a half, but I'll still get it out."

Then Mom started laying out the pattern pieces, full of confidence and determination. But she didn't just fold the fabric down the middle, lay out the pieces and cut. Not my mother!

Instead, she folded the fabric one way, and laid out a couple of pattern pieces, then folded it another way for the next few, and finally, squeezed the remaining pieces from the scraps that would be left over—if she had actually done any cutting.

But she was in her teaching mode, so instead of just cutting the thing out, she gathered up the pattern pieces, refolded the fabric into a nice little square, and handed the stack back to me.

"Your turn."

"Mom!" I moaned. "You already had it all laid out! Why didn't you just cut it?"

"Because you need the experience. So get going."

"*Experience*," I mimicked, making a face as I spread out the fabric and tried to remember what she'd just shown me.

"But you have to ease my pain by telling me another story," I insisted. Why not try to get something for myself out of the situation?

"What pain?" she snorted, with a very tiny, indulgent smile. She was used to my dramatics.

"The pain of having to figure this out all over again. So how about... how about telling me about what Lyndon was like as a kid?"

"What? You're back on that again?"

"Yes! C'mon, I need some *diversion*."

"Hmpf," she sniffed. "Well, I didn't know him as a kid."

"Yes, but you must have known certain things about him. Tell me those."

She sighed, settled herself in a chair where she could watch what I was doing, and thought for a moment.

"All right, let's see. He was born on a farm in 1918 to a big family—I think there were four boys and two girls, and he was number four."

She pointed to one of my pattern pieces. "That's got to be on the straight grain. You've got it crooked."

I made a face and straightened it.

"Anyway, they left the farm because his father got a job working for a newspaper in St. Paul—I'm pretty sure he was a linotype setter. Whatever he did, I know he worked nights and slept during the day, so the family didn't see him much. And that meant his mom pretty much raised the kids on her own."

I was still struggling with her crazy layout pattern.

"Do I fold it *this* way now?"

"Yes, fold it the wide way."

"Hmmm. Okay, so what was his mom like?"

She sighed.

"Well, I didn't really know her all that well. She always struck me as kind of cold and fussy." To illustrate, she added, "She was a card-carrying member of the Women's Christian Temperance Union."

If that had any significance, it was lost on me.

"What's that?"

"A bunch of old ladies who are dead set against alcohol."

"Oh."

"But she wasn't cold to Lyndon; she was crazy about him. Out of all of her kids, he was her favorite."

"Really? He told you that?"

"Yes. And I'm sure it was true." Her face softened a little as she remembered.

"He was very sweet, a real congenial sort of guy, very considerate and, you know, diplomatic. I think he was a sympathetic ear for his mother. She probably got lonely raising those kids by herself, and I think he sort of became her friend."

I held up the scraps I had left over.

"Do you *still* think I can get two pieces out of this?" I asked incredulously.

**Lyndon Raff, 21, shortly before he met Mom**

25

She got down on her hands and knees, folded the material this way and that, and showed me exactly how each piece would fit. I followed her instructions, and when I finished cutting out that last pattern piece, I was triumphant.

"Ta-da!" I shouted, throwing it into a pile with the others.

"Good job, kiddo," Mom enthused. "See, you can do it!"

Then, as she helped me gather up the scraps and wayward pins, she said lightly, almost too lightly, "By the way, don't mention any of this stuff to Dad, okay?"

"What stuff?"

"You know, about Lyndon."

"Why not?"

She sighed.

"Let's just say he doesn't want to hear about it. So don't mention anything. It'll be our little secret."

"Okay," I said, shrugging.

As if I ever mentioned anything to him anyway.

That evening Dad happened to be away for a business meeting, and since Dawn was off in the mountains working as a camp counselor, Mom and I were alone for dinner, which was a rarity. To celebrate, we were having sweet omelets topped with maple syrup, something Dad would never have tolerated.

"Okay, so anyway, back to my favorite subject," I began. "How did you and Lyndon start dating? You met him at camp, came home, and then what?"

This time, instead of giving me one of those doubtful, semi-suspicious looks, she actually smiled a little. Either she realized that trying to put me off was useless or she was actually starting to enjoy these little trips into the past.

"Well," she said slowly, sipping her coffee and thinking back. "I guess the first thing we did was tour the Hamline campus. He lived right across the street and had gone there for four years. So he knew the place inside out. And it didn't cost him anything, which was very important during the Depression."

"What year was it?"

"1939."

"Whew, ancient history! Okay, you saw the school. And then you just started dating all the time?" I was still trying to figure out how romances worked.

"Yes, we were together a lot that summer. He really showed me around St. Paul, which was great since I'd just moved there and didn't know much about the city."

"What kinds of things did you do?"

"Well, we went to Como Park, which is this great big beautiful park right in the middle of the city with a really nice lake where you could go ice skating in the winter and canoeing on summer evenings."

Her gaze softened.

"In Minnesota, it stays light until about ten o'clock in the summer, and the light is really soft and kind of golden. I remember never wanting to go home on those nights."

Then suddenly, she came back to earth and was all business.

"You're not going to waste that omelet, are you?" she asked a little sharply, eyeing my plate.

I hurriedly stuffed a bite into my mouth and tried to keep the story going.

"And what else did you do that summer?"

Mom leaned back in her chair, trying to remember.

"We liked to dance," she said brightly. "There was a place called the Coliseum Pavilion that had a great big dance floor that was smooth as glass, and we'd go swing dancing. You know, like, 'jeepers creepers, where'd you get those peepers?'" She bounced a little in her chair as if she was dancing, holding up an index finger and wagging it back and forth.

"Mom!" I guffawed through a bite of omelet. "That's so *corny*!"

"What's wrong with it? Here's another one," she said gaily, jumping to her feet and pulling me with her. She held my hands in hers and we bebopped around the kitchen as she sang, "In the mood, it's you I'm missin', in the mood, oh boy, I want that kissin'! Baby dontcha know it that I'm in the mood now!"

I scream-laughed the entire time and finally yelled, "Ugh! Enough of the Swingin' Years!"

Then she stopped, which actually made me a little sorry. We didn't have many opportunities to dance around the kitchen like that.

As we cleared the table and caught our breath, I tried to keep the mood going.

"Any other fun times that you can remember?"

"Oh, what *did* we do anyway? Hmmm. He and I spent a lot of time at Hamline Sweet Shop eating ice cream sundaes. And of course, we went to the movies; Hamline Theatre had double features. But if we wanted to see something in Technicolor, woo-hoo, the big thing back then, we went to the Centre Theater. That's where we saw '*The Wizard of Oz*' and '*Gone with the Wind*.'"

"That's when those movies came out?"

"Yep, 1939. It was a big year."

It was obviously a big year for her, anyway.

My World History class in summer school was excruciatingly dull—that is, until we got to World War II. Although I didn't know a thing about the war, except that it involved Nazis, I suddenly had a connection to it—it was the war that took Lyndon away from Mom. And believe it or not, that was enough to get me to read all of the assigned sections and stay pretty interested.

My paper, however, was on the most boring topic in the universe: the events of 1941 that prompted the U.S. to enter World War II. Ugh. Normally, I would have half-copied a bunch of stuff from the encyclopedia and dashed the whole thing off as fast as possible. But this time I discovered a way to get interested and stay interested. I just kept asking myself, "What were Mom and Lyndon doing while the country moved toward war?"

I found that I could actually keep myself from falling into a stupor while working on my paper by imagining things like this:

In January Mom and Lyndon were holding hands, ice skating happily on beautiful Como Park Lake, while the Germans blasted England from the air, killing 40,000 British civilians and damaging or destroying more than a million homes.

In February Mom was breezing through her mid-year calculus exams at Hamline with no sweat at all, while German U-boats tried to starve the Brits into submission by sinking hundreds of Allied merchant ships loaded with food and other supplies that were headed for England.

In March Mom and Lyndon were gobbling hot fudge sundaes at Hamline Sweet Shop, while FDR signed the Lend-Lease Act, which allowed the U.S. to support the Allied forces without actually committing to the war.

In April the two of them were boogying to Glen Miller's "In the Mood" at the Coliseum Pavilion, while the Nazis used a combination of speed, surprise, and brutal force called the "blitzkrieg" strategy to take over Norway and Denmark.

In May Mom and Lyndon were munching buttered popcorn and watching *"The Wizard of Oz"* at the Centre Theatre while Hitler's forces took over the Netherlands and Belgium.

And in June, as the pair celebrated two years of "going steady," France fell to the Germans, and the Nazis occupied Paris.

Naturally, Mom didn't tell it to me like that, but I figured it was probably pretty close to the truth.

30

Whatever! At least it got me to focus long enough to get an A on my silly paper.

What she did tell me about that time was that she hadn't really paid much attention to what was going on in Europe. The news was bad, but like most people in the U.S., she thought it was Europe's problem, and we shouldn't get involved. Nobody really wanted to go to war. But by the time the summer of 1941 rolled around, the ominous news arriving daily from Europe was making the situation harder and harder to ignore.

Things got even more intense in the fall. At the beginning of November, Roosevelt put the Coast Guard under the control of the Navy, which was a clear preparation for war. By Thanksgiving the mood throughout the country had become unbearably tense.

And yet, it wasn't the craziness in Europe that finally got us into the war—it was Japan. In 1941, after trying to conquer China for four years, the Japanese were about to invade Thailand, Burma, and some other Southeast Asian countries and wanted the U.S. to stay out of the way. So they decided to do something huge— something so destructive that our navy would be completely crippled and we'd be scared off for good.

That "something huge" occurred on December 7 when the Japanese bombed our naval base at Pearl Harbor, Hawaii, killing thousands of sailors, soldiers, airmen, and Marines, and severely damaging the U.S. Pacific fleet.

Mom told me the Japanese thought we were so weak and resistant to war that we'd just give up.

31

Instead, we came after them with a vengeance.

∞

"Sure, I remember the day Pearl Harbor was bombed! Who wouldn't?" Mom exclaimed when I asked her about it.

She was simultaneously folding laundry and standing over me while I ironed Dad's shirts, a tedious chore that I hated, although it brought me 25 cents a pop. She knew I was inclined to slop through it, though, and was making sure I didn't.

"Now don't put a crease in the outside of those sleeves. You need to refold," she reminded me.

"I know, I know," I said impatiently, refolding the sleeve and clamping the iron onto it. "So, what do you remember?"

"I remember that my mother and I had gone to church that morning," she said matter-of-factly, "so we didn't hear anything about it until we got home. But once we walked into the house, I got a load of my father's face and knew something was *really* wrong. He looked like somebody had just punched him."

Sitting close to his old Kellogg radio, head cocked toward the speaker, Grandpa had turned to them in alarm and shouted, "They've bombed our Navy in Hawaii!"

"The first thing I thought," Mom said in a bewildered tone, "was 'Hawaii'? What's *our* Navy doing in Hawaii?' I couldn't imagine what he was talking about."

Drawing closer to the radio, they learned that the Japanese Navy had pulled off a sneak attack on Pearl Harbor, home to almost the entire U.S. fleet in the Pacific. It was so horribly destructive and unexpected that everybody was outraged.

Not only had the Japanese attacked Pearl Harbor, but they had also assaulted Malaya, Hong Kong, Guam, the Philippines, Wake Island, and Midway Island. Some 2,400 sailors, soldiers, and civilians had been killed, and the U.S. Pacific fleet dealt a crippling blow.

"What did you do next?" I asked, horrified.

She laid a folded towel into the laundry basket and sighed.

"I remember that when Lyndon came to my house that afternoon, we just looked at each other in disbelief." She shook her head sadly. "It was like the world had turned upside down. We didn't know what to think."

She picked up another dish towel, folded her arms across it, and held it against her torso as she remembered.

"He said, 'Let's just walk,' and then he tucked my hand into the crook of his arm. We ended up at Hamline Sweet Shop, where we huddled in a booth with friends and listened to those horrible radio announcements about the death toll and the devastation.

The bad news just droned on and on, and finally Lyndon couldn't take it anymore. He stood up, grabbed me by the hand, and said, 'C'mon, let's get out of here. I don't like the music they're playing.' And then we walked home without saying a word."

The following morning, Monday, December 8, the students at Hamline were called together for a special assembly.

"There were several hundred of us there," Mom

33

remembered, "all of us sitting quietly in the auditorium and listening to a radio broadcast of President Roosevelt's speech to Congress. You've heard it—it's the one when he called December 7 'a date which will live in infamy.' And then he said something like, 'As commander in chief of the Army and Navy, I've ordered that all measures be taken for our defense.'"

In other words, we were at war with Japan.

"I remember having a sinking, numbing feeling," she said, shuddering as she recalled that terrible day. "There we were, a whole assembly of people, and not a sound. Just a sickening, depressing silence."

Three days later, Germany and Italy declared war on the United States. World War II was underway.

CHAPTER TWO

# Fly Boy

Many years later, Mom showed me a picture of herself and her family that was taken in December 1941. Her brother, my Uncle Ted, a newly-commissioned officer in the Navy, was home for Christmas. He'd quit his job earlier that year to join the Navy, thinking it would pay a lot better than his current job of teaching math to junior high school kids. After a stint in Midshipmen's school, he was in the process of wrapping up his training when, out of the blue, Pearl Harbor was bombed. There was just enough time for him to make a quick trip home for Christmas before heading off to "torpedo school," after which he would be assigned to a destroyer.

Grandma, like most mothers at the time, was terrified at the prospect that her son might never return. She wanted a family photograph made—possibly the last one ever taken of everybody together—and insisted the family get dressed up and take a trip to the local photographer's studio.

Not surprisingly, the picture reveals a pretty solemn little group. The only one who smiled even a little was Ted, who looked squarely into the camera and seemed to welcome the challenge he was about to face. Mom, a serious-faced twenty-year-old, was serenely beautiful but somehow detached, like she didn't really believe anything terrible was about to happen. My rough-and-tumble Grandpa appeared ready to take on anything and anybody, as evidenced by his clenched fist. Only one of them, my grim-faced, stoic Grandma, seemed to understand that the war was about to take a toll on them, and maybe a heavy one. But there wasn't a blessed thing she could do about it. The war had commandeered all of their lives.

**The Ostrom family, on the brink of war—December 1941**

"What about Lyndon?" I asked. "Did he run right out and sign up for the Army?"

I'd heard that all the young guys were furious about Pearl Harbor and dying to get out there and defend their country.

"No, he waited until after the holidays," Mom recalled. "But right after New Year's, he went straight to the Army Air Forces recruiting station and signed up."

Years later, I would find out it was on January 13, 1942, just five weeks after the attack on Pearl Harbor, that Lyndon joined the hordes of other would-be enlistees and applied for the U.S. Army Air Forces Aviation Cadet program. He knew absolutely nothing about flying planes; in fact, he'd never even been inside one. But according to Mom, being a pilot sounded exciting and fun to him, and a whole lot better than living in a foxhole or being stuck in the middle of the ocean hoping your ship didn't sink.

And while it was true that Lyndon was all fired up about doing his patriotic duty and protecting those at home, Mom confided that those weren't the only reasons. At the time, even though he'd graduated from college more than two years earlier, he was working in the warehouse at Montgomery Ward department store with no real job prospects on the horizon. And during those last dreary years of the Depression, life in St. Paul had slowed to a crawl. For most guys, there were only three exciting things to do: drive too fast, drink too much, and try to make time with your girl. As far as I know, Lyndon didn't do any of them.

But by joining the military, he'd get a chance to visit exciting new places, meet interesting people, and do all kinds of things he'd never dreamed of. Not to mention the fact that, finally, his hard-won college degree would come in handy. In the military, college graduates automatically had the chance to become officers, leaders among men. So almost overnight, a lowly warehouse clerk could become someone important.

With high hopes, Lyndon threw his hat into the ring and went through a series of interviews and examinations. Within two weeks, he got the verdict: the Army Air Forces had accepted him, and he was to report for basic training at Minter Field in central California in two weeks. With daytime temperatures of about 63 degrees right in the middle of winter, it sounded like a pretty good gig to a Minnesota boy.

Mom told me this story while we were strolling under a tangle of two-hundred-year-old California oak trees at Descanso Gardens, a beautiful place we liked to go whenever Dad loosened his iron grip on our car.

"Was it sad saying goodbye to Lyndon?" I asked, wondering what it was like to watch your boyfriend go off to war.

She wasn't about to wallow in any of that.

"Yes," she said shortly. "But that's just the way it was. Practically every girl I knew in those days was saying goodbye to her husband or boyfriend."

"So, no big deal?"

"Well, of course, it was a big deal! But, really, it would have been worse if he *hadn't* gone."

I cocked my head and gave her a look. At the moment we were smack in the middle of the Vietnam War, and going was a lot worse than not going.

"Back then, *everybody* went," she explained. "It was expected. If a guy stayed home, people said mean things to him like, 'What's the matter with *you*? Are you 4-F or something?' People thought he was a wimp."

Okay, that made sense. Nobody wanted to be a wimp.

"What did you do after he left?"

"I went to school! That didn't change. I took classes and did my work and went out with my girlfriends."

Her voice softened a little when she added, "And I wrote letters—lots and lots of letters."

Almost every day, as it turned out. And sometimes she sent him care packages full of homemade cookies.

"Sounds like a lot of work," I commented.

"It was. But I really wanted to do it—it was my way of helping him through."

∞

Minter Field was not much more than a two-week pit stop where the guys gave up the last vestiges of civilian life and received their preliminary training. Basically, it was a holding tank for some nine hundred cadets, who were then farmed out to one of ten primary training fields to begin their actual flight training.

39

It was also the place where Lyndon wrote his first letters home. Years later, I would wish with all my heart that I could have read some of those letters Mom wrote to Lyndon during the war, and the ones he wrote to her, but not a single one exists. I asked her once what became of them, and she said, "Oh, they're long gone. Once I remarried, it seemed pointless to keep them."

Then, just a few years ago, lightning struck. Long after Mom had passed on, quite extraordinarily, I gained access to a cache of twenty-eight of Lyndon's wartime letters. Although not one was written to Mom, they gave Lyndon a voice, a point of view, feelings, and a life.

And as I read his scribbled observations, explanations, requests, and jokes, a portrait of the young pilot who married my mother slowly began to emerge.

There was the lonesome boy far from home:

*... this has been a rather lonely day. Easter Sunday has always been a busy day with candy and flowers and new hats and suits for some. But it's just another day around here ...*

There was the serious, determined student:

*Got a 97 in Navigation test, 95 in a Math test, but a 60 in an Airplane Structure test. That one I didn't do so well in was a surprise test, but I'll be ready for him next time.*

There was the annoyed, possessive older brother:

*... I do not want Willis to get ahold of either my suit or this coat because he'd misuse it for sure.*

There was the chastened soldier:

*I had to "walk the ramp" for ½ hour last Sunday ... because of dusty bed springs, dust above the door frame, and [a] crooked lamp shade. This Sunday I have to "walk" about 2 hours for an error on a report ...*

And there was the proud cadet:

*The cadet is the envy of most of the soldiers around here because of the quality and neatness of our uniforms, pay, life we lead here and the way the "girls go for cadets."*

Then he added modestly:

*"I haven't noticed any of the last item as far as I'm concerned, however—probably mostly*

41

*because I don't think I'm as interested in others
as I used to be.*

This last remark, so casually tossed off, was one of several he made about his growing feelings toward Mom. He didn't seem to get really serious about her until after he left home. But just six weeks into his training, he sent this request to his parents, along with a money order:

> *Sometime in the near future have Nina and
> possibly her folks over for a dinner and use this
> to buy some more ice cream and make it a pretty
> good meal ... If I were home now, I'd do it myself,
> but when I was home I didn't think as I do now.*

Ten days later, he made this cryptic announcement:

> *Even though I couldn't be there last Sunday, I
> wanted you all to know now, more or less
> officially, that there's someone else I miss not
> seeing. I didn't realize I would until I got out
> here, and now it'll be quite a while before I get
> back and can make up for the time I wasted.*

Absence had definitely made his heart grow fonder—and more serious!

In letters that followed, Lyndon strongly encouraged his parents to get to know his girlfriend better, beginning with:

*Nina has several pictures that I've sent her ... why don't you ask her to stop in some afternoon or evening with them?*

In another, he gently nudged:

*She's been gone on a choir trip but should be home now.*

In a third, he hinted:

*She's a little shy and bashful probably but now that it's quiet around there ... maybe it'll be a little easier to get better acquainted.*

The guy was pushing hard to forge a connection between his parents and his girlfriend—and the sooner, the better.

Besides the windfall of letters, I also got my hands on a copy of Lyndon's Army personnel file. And with these two sources, plus some of my own research, I was able to get a pretty clear idea of what Lyndon was doing in 1942 and '43.

**Lyndon arrives at basic training – February, 1942**

In February, shortly after settling in at Minter Field, he wrote that he and his fellow cadets were doing "a little drilling and a lot of sitting around," the major activities being getting shots, listening to lectures, and taking tests. He worried about not making it through the program, but hung on to a positive attitude:

*I'm just over the edge on this physical and may*
*slip on any one of a number of things. OK now*
*for awhile though. About 50% to 70% of the*
*fellows as far as I am never get to be pilots or*
*[get] their commission, but I hope I'm one of*
*those others.*

There were other details to deal with as he made the transition from private citizen to soldier. Once he received his uniforms, he bundled up the last of his civilian clothes and sent them home to his parents, along with lists of things he wanted to save or give away. Then, almost as an afterthought, he added:

*Sometime you will be getting my U.S. life*
*insurance policy. Look it over if you want to and*
*then send it out here—and if you don't*
*understand it I'll try to answer any questions*
*about it. ($10,000 isn't hay.)*

He was referring to the $10,000 life insurance policy issued to all soldiers—just one more bit of housekeeping he needed to attend to before moving on.

According to his file, Lyndon started primary training ("ground school") in March at Hancock Field in Santa Maria, California, where he went through nine hard weeks of drilling, plus long hours in the classroom studying navigation, airplane structure, engines, and the use of aeronautical charts. Evidently, the "washout" rate at this point was huge. Lyndon reported that:

> *... the school graduates about 33 percent of its students or less—the lowest percentage of any primary school in California.*

This meant that by the end of the nine weeks, two-thirds of the cadets would be out on their ears, a sobering thought.

In the meantime the fun was about to begin. During primary training, cadets were required to put in sixty hours of flight time in a two-seater training plane, so Lyndon was finally going to get into the pilot's seat and start flying! He would be practicing take-offs and landings, straight-and-level flight, turns, climbs, and descents. If it sounded risky, well, Lyndon didn't seem to think so, assuring the folks back home that the danger was:

> *... practically negligible. If anything did happen or if you hear of any accident in a place such as this, it was almost for sure callousness on the student's part. Trying to show off...*

Apparently all went well because in May, according to the file, he moved on to Stockton Field to practice navigation, cross-country flying, and flying in formation. Pilots-in-training also started soloing within their first two weeks and were soon flying up to six hours a day.

At the end of this nine-week training period, cuts were made. Those who weren't knocked out of the program completely were divided into four groups: pilots, bombardiers, navigators, and radio operators. Lyndon, that lucky guy, not only stayed in the program, but made it into the pilot category.

In advanced training, the newly-designated pilots learned to fly the Curtiss-Wright AT-9, a powerful twin-engine plane that flew and felt like combat aircraft. The AT-9, which was notoriously difficult to control, had actually been designed to be less stable for teaching purposes. The theory was if you could handle the AT-9, you could handle anything.

When flying this plane, rookie pilots learned how to respond if an engine failed in midflight or, even worse, during take-off. One very important technique, practiced over and over again, was "feathering" a dead engine—that is, adjusting the prop blades so they paralleled the direction of flight. This reduced the drag and kept the prop from spinning in the wind. If an engine suddenly went out, feathering it might be the only way of maintaining the plane's altitude, making it an absolutely essential skill for any pilot.

**Pilot training—Spring 1942**

In the middle of going through Lyndon's file and learning about the training of World War II pilots, I made myself stop and think about what it all meant. During his seven months of training, Lyndon had managed to rise to every challenge and pass every test. Other cadets were constantly being washed out of the program, and most of those who stayed became bombardiers, navigators, or radio operators, not pilots. So, what was it about Lyndon that allowed him to win over and over again and eventually become a pilot?

Andy Rooney, of *60 Minutes* fame, may have come up with the answer in his book *My War*. As a war correspondent during World War II, Rooney had the chance to get to know plenty of pilots, and he described them as "natural leaders" and "... almost always the most capable, most intelligent, and most determined to accomplish their mission of anyone on board." He added, " They were in charge for a good reason."

The pilot not only controlled the plane; he was the superior officer in charge of everyone on board. The guy had to radiate power, confidence, and efficiency. Physically, Lyndon wouldn't have been an obvious choice, at 5'6" and 130 pounds. He also lacked the aggressive, Type A personality so characteristic of most pilots; virtually every description of his personality included the words "nice" and "sweet." Still, he'd always been a leader, even as a child, when he'd organized and motivated his five siblings, three of whom were older than he was. He must have had a lot more than his share of charisma and organizational ability, not to mention a very cool head.

Whatever the reasons, Lyndon was obviously a winner, and on August 27, 1942, he received his pilots' wings, along with a commission as a 2nd lieutenant. Next stop was Sedalia Army Air Field in Missouri, where he would learn the job he'd be doing overseas, flying C-47 troop carrier planes.

But instead of doing the town with his fellow cadets after graduation, he hopped on a train and headed straight to St. Paul to see his girl. They had been apart for nearly eight months, and he knew for certain that once the war was over, he wanted her to be waiting for him. In fact, he was so sure about it he had a diamond engagement ring in his pocket.

∞

Mom told me she barely slept once she knew Lyndon was on his way home. And when his old car pulled up in front of her house, and a handsome, tanned young Army Air Forces officer hopped out and loped up the walkway, she almost couldn't contain herself. She flew out the front door and straight into his arms, where they both laughed, cried, kissed, and held on to each other for dear life.

"It seemed like forever since he'd left," she recalled, "And once he came home, even though it was just for a week, we were going to squeeze as much living out of those days as we could."

Which is exactly what they did. They visited friends and family, went back to their old haunts, and talked endlessly about their future together. At night, they stayed out until the wee hours, swing dancing to "Chattanooga Choo Choo" and "Don't Sit Under the Apple Tree" and fox trotting dreamily to "I Don't Want to Walk Without You" at hot spots like the Coliseum Pavilion. Emotionally, they ricocheted from elation to heartbreak, from bliss to longing, and from manic energy to exhaustion. Those few stolen days were packed with a lifetime of emotion.

At the end of that crazy, wonderful, tumultuous week, they dragged their exhausted bodies back to Hamline Sweet Shop and flung themselves into a red leather booth. She was down in the dumps and trying hard to forget he would be leaving the following day. And that was the moment he decided to pull the engagement ring out of his pocket and ask her to be his wife.

In two seconds she shot from depression to elation, hardly able to contain her joy when he slid the ring onto her finger. When she could finally speak, she promised him she'd never take it off— and yes, *of course*, she would marry him!

Just eighteen hours later, he was on a train bound for Missouri, and she was sitting in Calculus class, busily scribbling notes and trying hard to give a damn about school. Back to reality. But whenever she glanced at the sparkling diamond ring on her left ring finger, she just couldn't stop smiling.

Lyndon had barely arrived at Sedalia Army Air Field when he scored yet another win. Right off the bat, the newly-commissioned troop carrier pilots were assigned to one of two categories, pilot or co-pilot, and once again, he landed in the top category.

The troop carrier pilots would train on the C-47 Skytrain, the "workhorse" of the Army Air Forces. Rugged, reliable, and versatile, this plane, the military version of the civilian Douglas DC-3, was the one most often flown by U.S. troop carrier pilots. It would play absolutely crucial roles in the D-Day Invasion and, later, the Berlin Airlift.

**C-47 Skytrain** *(courtesy USAAF)*

With its two 1,200 horsepower Pratt & Whitney engines, cargo hooks under the wings, reinforced fuselage floor, and large cargo door, the C-47 was used to carry troops, evacuate the wounded and even "snatch" stray gliders.

But mostly it was used to haul supplies: gasoline, bombs, ammunition, oil, food, engineering equipment, or anything else you could think of, often to far-off or hard to access destinations. While it wasn't a large plane, the C-47 could hold 28 soldiers in complete combat gear, 18-22 fully equipped paratroopers, or 14 patients on stretchers plus three nurses. It could also carry 6,000 pounds of cargo (7,000 in a pinch), including a 37 mm cannon or a fully assembled jeep. In other words, just about anything.

For Lyndon, flying the C-47 was a dream compared to the unstable AT-9 he'd wrestled with at Stockton Field. It was known as a "forgiving aircraft"—easy to fly and maintain, with a hardy construction highly resistant to battle damage and crashes. Many survivors of crash landings swore they owed their lives to the superior protection of this stalwart, dependable plane.

Pilot training included some fifty hours in the pilot's seat, flying in all kinds of weather and at all times of the day and night. The plane was stuffed to capacity with 6,000 pounds of sandbags to simulate the loads they would be hauling during battle conditions.

Then, to make matters more interesting, the pilots had to fly just 500 feet off the ground or even less. Low flying was a crucial skill for transport pilots as the C-47 was often used to drop paratroopers and supplies. The closer they got to the ground, the more likely it was that the drops would hit the target area.

For the same reason, the pilots also had to fly as slowly as possible, while being careful not to let plane stall.

The six-week training period was rigorous, exciting, and exhausting, and Lyndon found himself pushed to do things he never could have imagined when he was a warehouse clerk back in St. Paul. And when the training ended, he received his orders to report to Pope Field Air Force Base at Ft. Bragg, North Carolina – his final stop before going overseas.

But first, he had a two-week leave coming to him.

Mom told me he called her out of the blue from Missouri in early October, and the minute she answered the phone, he blurted out:

"Sweetheart, I'm coming home on leave in two weeks! Wanna get married?"

He didn't have to ask her twice.

CHAPTER THREE

# I Don't Want to Walk Without You

"To call it a whirlwind wedding doesn't begin to describe it," Mom said giddily. As we sat hemming dresses for my fall wardrobe, just the thought of her wartime nuptials made her smile and shake her head in disbelief.

"I had two weeks to plan my wedding. There was no time to make a wedding dress, and even if there had been, you couldn't find any nice fabrics during the war. So, my cousin lent me her dress and my mother altered it."

"And that's the white wedding dress you were wearing in that picture I found?"

"Yes. Then, some of my friends gave me their sugar and butter coupons so I could get a cake made. And we bought some flowers. That was about all you needed for a wartime wedding."

"What about the reception? Did you all guzzle buckets of champagne and dance up a storm to swing music?"

She looked at me like I was crazy.

"Are you kidding? We didn't even serve lunch! We just went next door to the Raff's house for cake and coffee."

"Not even a little *sip* of champagne?"

Then I remembered. "Oh yeah, Mrs. Raff was anti-alcohol."

"Yes. To say the least," she said drily.

"So, are there any pictures of you taken that day?"

It just wasn't going to seem real until I saw them together.

She left the room abruptly, and I could hear her rummaging around in the hall closet. When she came back, she was holding a black and white photo taken on the big day. They must have been outside the church because she wore a short black cape over her white dress.

In the picture, Mom smiled tenderly at the handsome young man in uniform standing beside her. But he looked straight at the camera with a big, wide grin. If he could have spoken, I imagined he would have said, "Finally, I got what I wanted!"

They both looked very, very happy. I hoped one day I would have a picture like that of myself, wearing a white dress and smiling lovingly at my fantastic new husband.

But that wasn't even the best part. Because she was Lyndon's wife, Mom got to travel with him to his new assignment in North Carolina, where they would be able to live together until he went overseas. Both of them were over the moon about it.

"Hey, but weren't you still in college?"

"I dropped out," she replied, without a hint of regret.

That was another little tidbit I'd never heard before! "

"Jeez, Mom, weren't Grandma and Grandpa furious?"

"Nope. Nobody said *anything* in those days if a girl left work or school to spend time with her man before he went overseas. That was considered A-OK."

**Wedding Day—Mr. & Mrs. Lyndon Raff**
**October 27, 1942**

So just a few days after the wedding, she found herself happily ensconced in an overnight train compartment with her brand-new husband, headed for North Carolina and a new life.

She said she was sitting there, just trying to wrap her mind around all that had happened to her, when Lyndon suddenly pulled a small box out of his pocket and handed it to her with a big smile.

"What's this?" she asked, genuinely surprised.

He'd already given her a beautiful double strand of pearls as a wedding present. How could he top that?

"Promise me that you'll wear this," he said, "especially when I'm away."

Inside the box, on a piece of white cotton, lay a silver pin: a pair of arching wings joined together by a tiny shield in the center.

"Your pilot's wings!" she cried.

He fastened the wings to her jacket and said, "Wear them right above your heart, and I'll always be with you."

That's when she pulled off her high school ring and put it on his little finger, the only one small enough to wear it.

It was a little bit of herself that she could send with him.

"After that," she told me, "I wore his wings all the time. I really believed that as long as I wore them, nothing bad would ever happen."

∞

**Honeymoon in Washington, D.C. - November 1942**

Mom remembered those golden months with Lyndon in North Carolina as one long celebration. Their honeymoon

59

consisted of a couple of stolen days in Washington, D.C., before his training started, when they raced from one famous site to another—places they'd always heard about but had never seen like the White House, the Capitol Building, the Washington Monument, and lots of museums. They even managed to zip over to Mt. Vernon and wander through George Washington's stately old home.

But all too soon it was back to the base for those last bits of training before Lyndon was deployed.

They moved into a little two-bedroom house just thirty minutes from Pope Field, which they shared with another pilot and his wife. What fun they must have had, two twenty-something couples, both newly-married, playing house for a few months before facing the reality and horrors of war. Married just two weeks, Lyndon wrote to his father about their new home:

> *It's a bit expensive but we're considered fortunate by many to have as nice a place as we do have. The girls have been busy buying things... such as a reasonable set of dishes and tableware, broom, shovel, dustpan, a couple small rugs, etc....*

Casting a little doubt on his twenty-one-year-old wife's culinary skills, he added:

*She talks of preparing a Thanksgiving dinner*
*but I think we'll eat at the Officer's Club...*

He then revealed something he would never have included in a letter to his mother:

*I'm certainly glad we can start our married life*
*away from St. Paul and the friends and relatives*
*there. If and when we ever get back to St. Paul*
*together to stay* [his emphasis], *we will have*
*been together long enough to not need any all-*
*too-well-meaning help.*

Finally, toward the end of the letter, he explained the reason for his sudden decision to get married:

*There were so many things in our favor all at*
*once that I couldn't see myself side-stepping this*
*any longer, and now I'm sure that if and when*
*my turn comes and we have to be separated for*
*a time, it'll be easier knowing and remembering*
*our married life together than if we were just ...*
*engaged without these weeks together.*

During the ten weeks that followed, Lyndon trained hard, hauling soldiers to military bases around the country, performing

61

night flights and resupplying missions, towing gliders under simulated combat conditions, and executing evacuations by air. Many of the flights were long and exhausting, and some required an overnight stay. But most of the time, Lyndon was able to get home in time to have dinner and spend the night with his new wife, which must have been thrilling for both of them.

Best of all, they were together for Christmas, which was a truly joyous one for both of them.

In a letter to his parents, Lyndon described his elation:

*Certainly had a nice Christmas here. The other fellow living with us didn't get home here from a trip to Milwaukee till 9:00 Christmas Eve and we thought he'd never come. We opened our things one at a time then. Had lots of fun too with a couple trick gifts. But the lounging robe and slippers Nina gave me were no trick. I gave her a dresser set ...*

*We had a couple chickens fried with real chicken gravy and mashed potatoes, etc. Quite a treat too. Can't get a decent meal in town at any price.*

*We've been burning scrap wood in the fireplace ... Have a fire in there now and it surely looks nice. The women have fixed a nice winter scene*

*on the mantel with a couple candles, and with the*
*tree lit it looks pretty nice in there ...*

*This year without actually being able to give or*
*receive much, I've still had even a little more, I*
*think, of the real Christmas spirit with a wife and*
*home here...*

*Just time enough for a shave and to bed now.*
*Usually get up about 6:30 these days. If I were a*
*bachelor I wouldn't have to get up till about 7:30.*
*(But it's worth it.)*

*Love,*
*Lyndon*

When I first read his letter more than seventy years later, I was surprised to see some very familiar handwriting at the bottom of the page—it was Mom's! There she was, weighing in with her own take on their newly-wedded bliss:

*It must have seemed strange to you people not to*
*be able to have your family with you this year.*
*Our Christmas seemed a little different too, but it*
*was so wonderful being able to be with Lyn. This*
*was our first Christmas and we really enjoyed it.*

*Whoops, excuse me, I just sneezed! A man with shaving soap all over his face—I guess it's my husband—just stuck his head in the door and told me to cover up. He watches me like a mother. Guess I'd better get ready for bed.*

*Nina*

I couldn't help wondering what her mother-in-law thought about *that* gleeful little message.

Mom said the orders they had been expecting and dreading came shortly after New Year's Day, 1943. On January 9, Lyndon was set to fly to West Palm Beach, Florida, along with the rest of his squadron, and there was no clue as to where they would be headed from there.

But obviously, it was somewhere overseas.

She recalled those last days before Lyndon left as a time when they finalized their plans for getting through the war.

"The plan was for me to go home, finish my degree, do some practice teaching, and get my teaching credential. That way, at least one of us would have a job once he got back."

As for where they would live, all they knew was it didn't have to be Minnesota.

California was nice, he told her. Maybe there.

One night during that time, Lyndon came home and announced that he'd made her the beneficiary on his life insurance policy, instead of his mother. While you'd think this would happen automatically once a soldier married, apparently that wasn't the case. Mom, who didn't like thinking about insurance policies and the reasons she might need one, just said, "Oh, okay," and changed the subject to something more pleasant.

The night before he left, the two of them sat on the floor in the living room surrounded by half-packed boxes and lamented that their time together was coming to a close. But both felt sure that their parting would only be temporary.

"We'll have all the time in the world to be together someday," he promised, as he held her close. She snuggled deeper into his arms and wished they could forget about the war and just disappear together.

Then, after a long and sleepless night, they got up early and said goodbye at the door. The squadron would spend the day at the base putting everything in order, then get an early start the following morning.

After that, who knew what would happen?

The other girl who lived in the little rented house was in the same situation as Mom. Her husband was also being deployed, and she was getting ready to move back home with her parents. Together, the two girls packed their belongings and got ready to leave.

"It was so depressing," Mom recalled.

That is, it was until one of them came up with a crazy plan to see their guys one last time. The squadron wasn't taking off until the following morning, so why not get up really early, dress to the nines, and go to the base to see them off? Both girls were instantly enthralled with their impulsive, romantic plan. It would be great fun, and the guys would love it!

Many years later, Mom smiled ruefully when she told me this story.

"I suppose it was a silly idea," she admitted. "I do know that once we got there, the guys weren't all that happy to see us."

"Why not?" I demanded. "It's so romantic!"

"Oh, who knows? They probably thought we'd already said our goodbyes and they didn't want to go through it all again. All I know is we *really* wanted to see them off. And that's what we did."

So Mom managed to grab a few more precious moments with Lyndon before he took off for Florida and destinations unknown.

It was the last time she ever saw him.

## CHAPTER FOUR
# Off to War!

It was an incredible sight to see: twelve C-47 transport planes, stuffed to the gills with the 1st Troop Carrier Squadron and all their gear, roaring down the runway at Pope Field and blasting off into impossibly blue skies.

In a letter to his father written from West Palm Beach the following day, Lyndon reported that the planes flew in three inverted V-shaped rows all the way to Florida, and he was in the "lead ship," co-piloting for the squadron commander. Then he added:

> *Still don't know where we'll end up, but rumor is still strong that it may be India by the long way around ...*

The rumor turned out to be spot-on: they were indeed bound for India as part of the Air Transport Command located in the China-Burma-India Theater. Their purpose was to help the Chinese fend off Japanese invasions by providing them with desperately needed supplies.

After four years of pounding the Chinese, Japan had managed to cut off all land and sea routes to China. Now the only way to deliver supplies to that country was by air, and that meant flying straight over the Himalayas, home to the famous Mt.

Everest, from Allied air-bases in India to Kunming, China. The guys who performed this feat called it "flying the Hump." And this was the way they delivered literally everything the Nationalist Chinese army needed—which amounted to some 777,000 tons of supplies by the end of the war.

When Mom told me about Lyndon's assignment flying the Hump and what it entailed, I was incredulous.

"He flew all that stuff over Mt. Everest?"

"Well, not over that one, but he did have to fly over some huge mountains, and there were terrible winds and storms. Some transport planes even got shot at by Japanese fighter planes."

"Yikes."

"Yes. It was really dangerous."

And that was an understatement. To this day, flying the Hump, which claimed the lives of 1700 men and close to 600 planes by the end of the war, is still considered the most dangerous feat ever assigned to air transport.

Surprisingly, Lyndon's letters mentioned very little about his undoubtedly harrowing trips over the Hump. Instead, he mostly described his new home at the air-base in Chabua, in India's state of Assam. Lyndon, an officer, lived in a bamboo hut instead of a tent like the enlisted men. Officers also had "bearers," servants who did their laundry and other odd jobs.

Still, life was far from luxurious. Insects, Lyndon wrote, flew and crawled into everything, and anyone who didn't wrap up in mosquito netting at night was eaten alive. Tigers and leopards lurked in the nearby jungle, and hyenas and barking jackals plagued all but the soundest of sleepers.

Most unnerving of all, though, were the cobras that slithered into huts and tents, took up residence in beds and drawers, and scared the wits out of just about everyone. In a letter to his brother Bill, Lyndon reported:

> *The Doc shot a cobra the other night outside our barracks and many other snakes have been seen around here. Remember how "skittish" I used to be about snakes? Well, I still am, and have my .45 handy most all the time to use if and when I ever stop running after seeing one of those things!*

The biggest problem, however, was the food, which was almost always either C-rations or Spam. The government was funneling most of its money to the European bases, so the guys in the China-Burma-India Theater just had to suck it up and eat whatever was available. And it wasn't much. Almost anything that tasted good was nonexistent on the base, including fresh fruit, bread, dairy products, and eggs.

Local food was out because of the high risk of food-borne illness. And *no one* dared to drink the local water without purifying it first.

Fortunately for Lyndon, the pilots usually didn't spend much time on the base. In fact, the day after he arrived at Chabua, he took off on the first of several jaunts around India, transporting military supplies and personnel. And, to his delight, as an officer, he often stayed in nice hotels and ate at high-end restaurants.

**Lyndon (far rt.) and fellow pilots in Delhi, India, 1943**

For his inaugural trip, Lyndon flew a planeload of wounded men 1,750 miles to the port city of Karachi, and afterward enjoyed his reward, as evidenced in this letter to his parents:

*Stopped at Delhi going back and spent a swell night there. Had to stay in a hotel... Took a real shave for a change ...*

*At the hotel ... we were treated like men again... we have a "bearer" (valet), a native who looks after our personal wants, etc. ... They'll heat water, press and/or launder clothes, shine shoes, make bed (poorly usually), sew buttons, etc.*

*...Served us tea in bed 10 min. before our call to be awakened. A good tho small fireplace in each room... and plenty of hot water. I bet I soaked for 30-40 minutes.*

Trips like these were a real boon for Lyndon. Besides gaining valuable piloting experience and enjoying the royal treatment, the flights themselves were relatively safe and gave him opportunities to explore the cities and sights of India.

Decades later, while in the middle of reading his letters, I came across an old receipt for an evening bag he'd purchased from a store in Delhi on that trip.

On the back, he'd scrawled:

*Bought Nina a velvet silver & gold hand-embroidered bag that looked nice even to me ...*

71

*This outfit's head office, if they had a few modern showcases, would put any place I've seen in the U.S. to shame.*

But all too soon, it was back to Chabua, where he would begin flying the notorious Hump. In an attempt to reassure his folks that he was safe, Lyndon wrote:

*I haven't been "Over the Hump" yet as I was sent right back on this special mission, but as soon as I get back up there I'll start in. It'll be a little shorter but at a higher altitude than some of our regular runs in and out of Pope.*

In other words, no big deal.

∞

The day after Lyndon's deployment, Mom jammed as many of her newly-purchased household items as she could into two suitcases and caught the train back to St. Paul. Goodbye to married life; hello to the old grind.

"There I was, a 'married lady' back in my parents' house, living in my old teenage bedroom. It was like nothing had ever happened," she said, shaking her head.

We were almost finished with my pesky fall wardrobe—to the point of tacking down facings and adding buttons.

"So, then what?"

"Well, of course, I had to go back to school and finish my degree. I actually took twenty units that spring. Ugh!"

"Well, that's what you got for running off and getting married!" I joked.

"Yeah. Hmpf."

I felt for her, though. Cinderella was definitely home from the ball.

"That was it? Just studying and waiting around?"

"Pretty much. The first thing I did, though, was get a picture taken of myself. He'd asked for one."

"What picture?"

"You've seen it—it's the painted one."

I knew what she was talking about; it was in our family album. Throwing my sewing aside, I dragged the album out of the closet and flipped through the pages until I found it.

There it was, a classic 1940s colorized portrait of my very beautiful mother. Her skin was bronzed, with rouge and lipstick painted on, and eyelashes painstakingly drawn in. She wore the double strand of pearls that Lyndon had given her as a wedding present as she looked dreamily into the distance.

I wondered what she was thinking. Was she imagining a wonderful future for herself: a husband back from the war, a home of her own, a career, children, all that good stuff?

**Nina Ostrom Raff, age 21 – 1943**

But when I asked her, she just snorted and said, "Oh who knows? I was probably just hoping the picture would look okay."

Then she turned back to the sewing machine and ran up a seam at breakneck speed. So much for romantic longings.

I don't know how much Mom knew about what it was like to be a Hump pilot. Lyndon didn't say much about it in his letters to his family, so I suppose it was the same in his letters to her. But years later, I would read about what Hump pilots went through during the war. And it was even more awe-inspiring and alarming than I'd imagined.

For a pilot based in Assam, flying the notorious 1,000-mile round-trip over the Hump always began the same way. At 4:00 a.m., someone from Operations stole into his hut, shook him awake, and whispered one word into his ear: China.

I could imagine Lyndon quietly gathering his shearling jacket, over-trousers, and boots, while trying not to wake his bunkmate, then making his way through the darkness to the Operations hut. There he would get his orders, review the route, pick up the cargo manifest, and say hello to his three-person crew: a co-pilot, a navigator, and a radio operator.

As the last of the cargo was being loaded (typically it was 55-gallon drums of gasoline, although C-47s also transported small vehicles, ammunition, heavy equipment, canned beans, trash cans, personnel, and, once, even a grand piano for Madame Chiang Kai-shek), Lyndon and his co-pilot would safety-check the plane inside and out while the others got settled on board.

The first big hurdle of the day, always, was simply getting off the ground. But clearing the nearby mountains could also put a pilot into panic mode. That's because Chabua is barely above sea level while the mountains around it soar as high as 10,000 feet.

Lyndon would really have to gun the plane's engines and point its nose toward the sky if he was going to clear those treacherous crags in just a few short minutes.

But as soon as he'd gained enough altitude, he would have a minute or so to enjoy the breathtaking view, especially once the sun began to rise. Then the ground below would become a patchwork of green tea plantations, rice paddies and jungle thickets sprawling over the Himalayan foothills like a soft, fuzzy green blanket.

Next, with engines at full-bore, Lyndon would struggle furiously to climb to the standard cruising altitude of 16,000 feet. And the higher the plane rose, the more uncomfortable it would become for those inside the cabin. At 10,000 feet, the crew would have to don oxygen masks to catch a decent breath and ward off searing headaches. And by the time they finally reached cruising altitude, the temperature inside the plane would have plummeted well into the frigid zone. If Lyndon was lucky enough to be flying a plane with hoses that delivered heat to the cockpit, he and his co-pilot could tuck those hoses inside their clothes and stay warm throughout the flight. They'd be in hog heaven. But everyone else on board would just have to suffer.

Just looking out the window at the glorious views of the Himalayas' snowcapped peaks, however, would lift everyone's spirits. The Himalayas are actually three huge belts of mountain ranges stretching over 1,500 miles in length and up to 250 miles in width. And each range is rife with jagged peaks, massive

IF MY HEART HAD WINGS

glaciers, and expansive, glittering snowfields. From high in the air, it must have looked like an ocean full of roiling, rocky whitecaps extending as far as the eye could see.

And then came the "fun" part.

When the peaks exceeded 16,000 feet (and several of them soared to at least 24,000 feet), Lyndon would have to guide the plane in between them, where winds became a major enemy. Turbulence reigned at all times of the year, with 100 to 200 mph winds screaming down the sides of mountains and eventually colliding with each other.

Flying through these crazy winds was like riding a bucking bronco. Some Hump planes actually flipped upside down, terrorizing both pilots and crew, who referred to their missions as "Operation Vomit."

And all along the route, Lyndon would have seen the remains of wrecked planes glinting in the sun on the rocky peaks below, the reason the route was often called "The Aluminum Trail." To keep from becoming a part of that trail, he would have had to use every trick he'd ever learned about piloting a plane.

But that's not all he had to face.

Huge cloud formations often blanketed the Himalayas, and Lyndon knew that flying straight through them was extremely dangerous. With no radio navigation aids or charts to guide him through, he could easily steer the plane straight into the side of a mountain.

**Flying the Hump in a C-47** *(courtesy USAAF)*

Yet flying above the clouds wasn't a great answer either. Above a certain elevation, ice would form on the plane's exterior, weighing it down and changing the airflow over the wings and tail. When this happened, the plane might suddenly drop 1,000 feet or more, or go into a nosedive.

While Lyndon struggled to keep the plane aloft, the panicked crew would tie themselves to the walls, kick the door open, and start tossing out drums of gasoline or any other heavy cargo until the plane finally lightened up enough to gain some altitude.

Finally, there was the constant threat of being attacked by Japanese Zero fighter planes. The Zeros were twice as fast and much more agile than the clunky, slow-moving transports. So if a Zero suddenly showed up, Lyndon's only hope would be to dive into the clouds and hide, even though the risk of crashing into the side of a mountain was huge.

By the time he finally made his way over the Hump and was cruising over the province of Yunnan toward the Allied air-base at Kunming, Lyndon must have breathed a huge sigh of relief. Yet the challenges were far from over. Heavy ground fogs often obscured the Kunming runway. And incoming planes could be stacked above the airstrip—sometimes as many as thirty at a time—circling and waiting for permission to land. If, by some miracle, Lyndon's plane didn't run out of fuel or crash into another plane, he could still blow out his tires on the airstrip, which was made out of crushed stone. Plenty of planes coming into Kunming met their end in crash landings.

Yet somehow, in spite of all these challenges, Lyndon would set his plane down safely in Kunming time after time. A sign hanging outside the Operations office said it all: "YOU MADE IT AGAIN. GOOD WORK!"

Then came the reward: eggs.

Kunming was literally the only place where aircrews based in India could get a breakfast of fresh eggs. A Chinese cook had created a makeshift restaurant out of the shell of an old plane where he specialized in cooking egg breakfasts. So this was the place where Lyndon and everybody else headed the minute they arrived.

"How do you want 'em, Joe?" the cook would ask the guys, using the only English sentence he knew. It didn't matter how they answered; he only knew how to scramble them. But nobody cared one whit.

∞

By the beginning of March, less than a month after he'd arrived, Lyndon had made nine round-trips over the Hump. By the end of March, he'd made eighteen. And while the stress ate away at many pilots, he didn't seem at all daunted by what he was doing. In one letter, he even talked about how lucky he was:

*I'd rather be in the Air Corps than any other outfit, and in the Air Corps rather be pilot than any other job. If I have to be overseas, I can think of few places I'd rather be than here and especially* [would] *rather be here than in No. Africa or the So. Pacific. And of all the types of airplanes and kinds of missions I could go on, I'd rather have this "little" C-47 and fly freight to where I do and over what I do ...*

The hardest part, apparently, was being separated from his wife. In a letter to his brother, who was serving stateside in the Army Air Corps, Lyndon wrote enviously about Bill's recent visit from his wife, Cheryl:

*I know how nice it was to have had your wife with you for awhile and too bad she can't stay down there more. But at least you're practically within call of each other and aren't way around the other side of the world from her.*

*I had a couple swell months* [with Nina] *so I'm not complaining, but I know now just why I want the "brass" in Wash. & Delhi to get this war over with and let me go home ...*

*Once I get back I'd like to take my wife and make a nice slow easy trip to the places I'd like to see again in the U.S.*

The following month, he wrote wistfully to Bill:

*I hear you're getting a furlough in a little while. Wish I could get home for awhile but don't expect to now until this mess is all over... There are about a dozen pilots going home tho they have been here 12-18 months. Hope I don't have to wait that long....*

*Well, when you get home be sure to say hello to my wife for me...*

Around this time, Lyndon made another attempt to foster a connection between the two women in his life:

*Mother, if you go home next summer as you mention, would you think it possible you and Nina and maybe Arlean could possibly go on a little trip together—to see Minnie & Art over some weekend for example?*

The guy wasn't going to give up easily.

## CHAPTER FIVE

# Goodnight, Wherever You Are

I was dying to wash my hands. The gooey bread dough I'd been kneading covered my palms and glued my fingers together. I could barely scrape the stuff off with a knife. We were still in the dog days of summer, but Mom had decided to bake bread and thought it was high time I learned how. So there I was, baking in August.

"Can't I add some more flour to keep it from sticking?" I asked my mother irritably, holding up my gunked-up palms. "And how much longer do I have to keep kneading?"

Mom eyed the dough expertly, then sprinkled it with a tiny bit of flour.

"You've got to knead for at least five minutes in order to develop the gluten. And don't overdo it with the flour," she warned. "Too much makes it dry."

Obviously, she'd been reading her food encyclopedia again. There was nothing she liked better than figuring out the reasons something worked—or didn't—whether it was food or anything else. Like a very talented fortune teller, the *Encyclopedia of Food Science and Technology* would reveal all: why your boiled broccoli turned olive green, why your soufflés fell flat, or your fudge crystallized. And, of course, why you'd better knead your bread dough for at least five minutes, unless you wanted undeveloped gluten.

This kind of stuff bored me silly. I'd rather make something wrong ten times in a row than look up an explanation in a book.

Desperate for something to occupy my mind while I wrestled with the sticky dough, I said, "So, tell me again about the time you worked for the CIA."

I pressed the heel of my hand into the dough, then folded it and pressed again, the way she'd taught me.

"The CIA?" Mom raised an eyebrow. "I never worked for the CIA. I worked at *Langley Field*, which is where the CIA is today. Hey, watch out, you're pushing flour onto the floor!"

"Oops. Okay, if it wasn't the CIA, what *were* you doing?"

"NACA hired me, the National Advisory Committee for Aeronautics. It's NASA today. Anyway, they were looking for women to do math calculations for their flight testing experiments because all the men were off to war. So they went around to the colleges looking for female math students who were about to graduate."

"And that was you."

"Yes, that was me."

She gathered up the dough, twisted it into two equal pieces, and handed both to me.

"Here, make a loaf shape out of each of these while I grease the pans."

Then she explained what they were doing at the place that was *not* the CIA.

NACA (referred to as "Langley" by virtually everyone) was charged with the task of designing and producing military planes, and they were under intense pressure to get faster and better planes into the air ASAP.

With a hugely increased workload and practically all of their male employees off to war, Langley was desperate for women who could do the mathematical equations and calculations necessary for the designing and testing phases. And they had to do them by hand, using slide rules, curves, and basic calculating machines because there weren't any computers back then. Those who performed these math calculations were called "computers," and their everyday tasks included reading, calculating, and plotting data gathered from the tests done in Langley's research division and wind tunnels.

Mom and two of her friends, Louise and Jo, had applied for the "computer" job when they were still in their senior year. And all of them were hired.

"The salary was terrific," she enthused. "$2,400 a year!"

It sounded pretty paltry to me.

"But it wasn't," she insisted. "Not in those days. It was *four times* what my dad made at the meatpacking factory. And twice what my brother was making as a teacher. You really couldn't beat it, especially if you were a woman."

The minute they graduated at the end of May, Mom and her two friends packed their bags and took off for the East Coast, giddy with excitement and looking forward to new adventures.

It wasn't all roses, of course. By the time the girls arrived, even the tiniest hole-in-the-wall had long since been rented out. They finally had to settle for a ramshackle old boardinghouse about forty minutes from Langley that was plagued with so many bugs and mice that they immediately nicknamed it "the menagerie."

The stone-faced landlady was just as cold and unpleasant as the house. But it was a roof over their heads, and there was a nearby bus line into town, so it would have to do.

Fortunately, the computer job was interesting and challenging, if a bit intense.

"We worked closely with the engineers," she told me. "They drew up the plans for the planes, the researchers did the testing, and we got the raw data. We did all the calculations and, boy, you'd better come up with the right answers, or everything could go haywire. I *always* rechecked my work at least three times before handing it over."

"Sounds like a ton of work," I sniffed. Ugh, who would want to do math problems all day long?

"It was work, all right," she admitted, "but it was also *fun*." Her gaze softened as she thought back to those days. "I always loved math because it's like a puzzle. And there I was at Langley, working on puzzles for a living and doing my part to bring the boys home sooner. What could be better than that?"

∞

I plopped the bread dough into the pans, slid them into the oven, and set the timer for fifty minutes. Then we escaped from the hot kitchen, carrying two glasses of iced tea and heading for the den.

"Did Lyndon know about your new job?" I asked, flopping on the couch and taking a big gulp of tea.

"Oh sure," Mom replied, leaning back in an easy chair and stretching her legs out on the ottoman. "I told him all about it in my letters. It was a big deal—my first real job, away from home, making money..."

"Did he ever call you?"

She gave me an incredulous look.

"He was *overseas*; there weren't any phone calls. But a couple of times, he did send me things."

She cocked her head girlishly and smiled.

"Like what?"

"Well, once he sent me a beautiful red Chinese robe."

"Are you kidding me? A Chinese robe! Did you wear it? Where is it?" I wanted to try it on that minute.

"No," she said, all traces of girlishness suddenly vanishing as she became her old practical self.

"It was way too fancy to wear around the house—and scratchy."

She took a sip of tea.

"I did like to take it out once in a while and look at it, though. It was floral brocade, very exotic and, well, very Oriental."

"So, where is it? Can I see it?!"

"Oh, who knows?" she sighed, with a wave of her hand. "It probably went to the Goodwill or something."

I was appalled.

"The Goodwill? *Mom!*"

Her fantastic husband sent her a robe all the way from China, and she gave it to the Goodwill?

She looked at me blankly, then laughed a little at my exaggerated dismay.

"Did he send you anything *else*?"

She must have held on to *something*.

"Yes," she said vaguely. "There was a very pretty evening bag that was made out of white satin with a lot of gold and silver embroidery on it. I think it was from someplace near the Taj Mahal."

"And where's the evening bag?"

Don't tell me you pitched it, I prayed.

"Oh, I don't know, Dene," she said, rubbing her forehead and suddenly seeming exhausted. "It's just gone. I haven't seen it in years."

∞

Shortly after Mom began working at Langley, Lyndon was given a well-deserved ten-day furlough, and immediately headed for a beautiful little resort town in the Himalayan foothills called Darjeeling. It was hugely popular with British and American soldiers, and British industrialists who were waiting out the war and were drawn there because of its cool air, masses of flowering plants, luxurious resort hotels, and spectacular views of the snow-laden Himalayas.

Hordes of soldiers regularly invaded Darjeeling to escape the heat and humidity of the jungles, stuff themselves with good food, and take in the views. They could also go to the movies, roller skate, ride ponies, chat with British industrialists, and try to make time with the daughters of these gentlemen at evening dances.

Apparently, Lyndon did all of these things, with the exception of the last one. In a letter to Bill about those glorious days in Darjeeling, he wrote:

*... had myself a swell time. Nice & cool up there. Went roller skating, pony riding, and dancing mostly for entertainment, also caught up on some good hrs. of bunk fatigue and ate some good food for a change.*

Then, in a paragraph meant only for his brother's eyes, he wrote:

*... there are plenty of "eager" white women for anyone that looks around. It was fun to look at, talk to, and dance with some of these but that's about as far as it went with me, tho some of the other guys said I was a sucker. I don't think so.*

89

This, of course, didn't mean that under the right circumstances he wasn't as lusty as the next guy, as evidenced later in the same letter:

*I got a kick out of a remark... [your wife] made about when you were home ... "All he wants to do is to look at the baby and hold my hand." Hmph, if that's all you did while at home, boy, you ain't no brother of mine!*

Eventually, of course, Lyndon had to come down the hill, but this time he reported to a new base, Dinjan, a new group, the 2nd Troop Carrier Squadron, and a new assignment.

Recently conducted psychological tests had found that the crews—and especially the pilots—flying the Hump for more than about six months were prone to "cracking up" from the stress. That's why Lyndon got a ten-day furlough and was given a new assignment.

His new gig involved airlifting supplies to guerilla fighters and to soldiers manning the air warning stations in the nearby Burma hills. Since most of the supplies were food, the pilots who made these runs were affectionately known as "biscuit bombers." It sounded pretty benign and a lot less dangerous than flying the Hump. But like almost every other task assigned by the military, it had its own dangers.

The biggest danger to the biscuit bombers was attacks from the deadly Japanese Zeros, which sometimes lay in wait for them, especially if they knew the locations of the drop zones. For this reason destinations were kept top secret until right before takeoff. And the transports usually took advantage of the cover of darkness, taking off before sunrise, even though their only guides were headlights, a compass, and the eyes of the pilot.

The next hurdle was finding the damned drop zone. Ground forces receiving the supplies cleared an area of jungle early in the morning, then laid out white silk parachutes spelling the code of the day. This way, the pilot would know everything was on the up and up and that he wasn't headed into a trap. But even though the pilot had the coordinates for the drop zone, it could be tough to spot it in the middle of that tangled jungle. Sometimes it took hours.

Then, when the drop zone was finally located, the pilot brought the plane as close to the ground as he could without crashing it, and slowed it to just above stall speed so the drops wouldn't fly off into the jungle. Not until he'd maneuvered the plane into the most advantageous position possible would he signal the crew to throw open the cargo door and start the drops.

At this point, three members of the crew shoved a stack of boxes to the edge of the doorway, while a fourth, the "kicker," lay on his back, put his feet against the bottom of the stack, and kicked it out the door. This process was repeated in a frenzy, with the goal of unloading as many boxes as possible while the plane cruised

91

over the drop zone. Often the pilot had to make several passes over a drop zone before an entire load could be delivered.

Things could easily go wrong. After slowing almost to idle, the plane's engines had to be pushed to the maximum to clear the nearby hills. Sharp turns around hilly terrain could send a crew member flying through the plane's open doorway. And flying low to the ground gave the pilot very little room to maneuver or make corrections. Biscuit bombing, then, was pretty serious business.

**Lyndon (far rt.) and fellow pilots in front of three C-47s**
**Assam, India -1943**

And that's what Lyndon did throughout the rest of the summer of '43 and into the fall; that, plus occasional trips over the

Hump. He didn't complain about it or even describe it his letters. Instead, he seemed to focus almost exclusively on some exciting but alarming news: his brother Bill was about to be sent overseas.

Bill, an air traffic controller, had written from Kelly Air Force base in San Antonio, Texas, that he was about to be deployed, although he didn't know where or when.

Suddenly, Lyndon was writing his brother letter after letter, asking for more details. In one, he was happy about the possibility of seeing Bill again, but still plenty worried:

*Sure would be fun to have you over here someplace, but I don't really want to wish any bad luck such as going overseas on you.*

Then he added, hopefully:

*If you came to just about any place in India or China we could get together sometime ...*

Apparently, Bill asked for a loan so he could "do the town" with his wife before being sent off and Lyndon replied:

*Letter received, money sent out today. I remember how much those last few weeks and days with Nina meant to me. So here's $50 for the duration ...*

Then he went back to his old pipe dream of seeing Bill in India:

*If your C.O. has anything to say about it, why don't you ask him to be sent to India? The hot summer will be over by the time you get here and the winter is rather comfortable ... if you get to __any__ field in India I'd get to see you sometimes and maybe oftener...*

But by late September, Lyndon still hadn't received word from his brother, and knew nothing of his whereabouts. He sent another anxious letter to Bill, this time admitting he was worried:

*I'd give a lot to know where you are now. It's been so long since I got that last letter of yours saying you'll be going overseas soon that there's a possibility you could be on a ship right here in this harbor.*

*If you get to India or China and ask enough Transport Pilots you're bound to soon run across some friend of mine or maybe even me ...*

*But I hope the best for you—that you and your family are still together someplace in the U.S. or if not, you've got a decent assignment someplace.*

On October 22, when there was still no word from Bill, Lyndon sent yet another letter. To lighten the mood and make a joke out of his own anxiety, Lyndon pretended he was piloting a plane and contacting the control tower at Kelly Field, where Bill was stationed, the last he heard.

With the kind of affectionate humor only guys engage in, he wrote:

> *KF Tower,*
> *From Army 0-729234—KF Tower!... Five miles out requesting landing instructions. KF Tower go ahead!—KF Tower, did you get that?*
>
> *Get your head out and answer these calls. What are you doing up there anyway? Giving some babe on the stroll the green light with the Aldis lamp, or reading some Flying Aces?*
>
> *Ever heard anything like that or don't you eager tower men there ever give them a chance? S'pose by now you're on your way on a transport and this will probably reach you by Christmas, but if so O.K.—Merry Christmas...*

*I'm saving a qt. of Seagrams V.O. for you if you ever get over here. We get a qt. ration once in awhile but I still can't like the stuff, tho I've tried...*

He followed this with a little brotherly ribbing, referring to an earlier letter he'd received from Bill:

*What are you trying to do? Rub it in with your last line, "I've got to go home to my wife and bed. Damn!!"*
*Just wait till I get back home and you're still overseas someplace. It'll be my turn then. But enough for now, Sargeant.*

*Lyndon*

It was the last letter he ever wrote.

CHAPTER SIX

# A Letter from Home

On the afternoon of October 29, Lyndon got orders to take a biscuit bomber sortie up into the Burma hills, not far from Dinjan. According to his Army personnel file, his plane took off at 1:30 p.m., which makes the trip seem like an afterthought; most supply runs were made in the early morning.

So, it's quite possible it was a spontaneous assignment—a sort of, "Oh hey, Lieutenant, you've got some time. Why don't you run this stuff up the hill real quick?" kind of thing.

The drop site was only seventy miles away, about thirty minutes of air time, and the weather that day was more than decent. In fact, it was CAVU—ceiling and visibility unlimited.

The C-47 was loaded and the crew assembled: pilot, co-pilot, navigator, radio operator, and four drop crew, plus an eighteen-year-old kid who apparently went along for the ride.

Then suddenly they were airborne, flying east above Assam, headed toward the green tangle of jungle covering the Burma hills. It was a beautiful time of day to cruise above the plains and thank God that monsoon season was finally over.

At 2:00 p.m., the Operations staff sergeant back at Dinjan made radio contact with Lyndon, who reported that all was well.

Finding a drop spot in the middle of that jumble of greenery was always a challenge, so the crew tried to help by coming to the front of the plane and peering out the cockpit windows, looking for tell-tale white parachutes spread out on the ground. Since some of the clearings were pretty small, several sets of searching eyes could be helpful.

And then somebody saw it: a bare spot on the near side of an upcoming hill, with white parachutes laid out. A valley lay just beyond the hill, where there would be plenty of airspace to bank the plane, double back, and bring it down low enough to the ground for an accurate drop.

Lyndon guided the plane above the clearing and out over the valley, made the turn, and headed back, coming in slightly below the level of the field, with just enough time to pull it up to the perfect drop-off level.

But suddenly, just as the plane approached the side of the hill, one of the engines began to sputter. According to an eyewitness, the choking and lurching continued for a couple of heart-stopping seconds until, at the worst possible moment, the engine cut out completely.

The terror on the faces of the pilot and crew was clearly visible to the soldiers on the ground. The plane was still desperately in need of altitude, but the area's strong downdrafts were pulling it in the wrong direction.

Using all of the skills and instincts honed during training, Lyndon feathered the dead engine in a desperate attempt to bring it back to life and gain those few crucial feet of altitude. And for a brief moment, he was successful: the motor suddenly burst into life for several seconds. But it was already too late.

The plane banked sharply to the left; a clear indication that the left engine had failed. Then the left wing snagged the top of a tree, sealing the fate of all on board. The plane flipped over, hit the ground, and, like a child's pinwheel, cartwheeled down the side of the hill. It crashed into a wash some 200 yards below and exploded into a ball of fire.

∞

The Operations office of the 2nd Troop Carrier Squadron tried in vain for more than two hours to contact Lyndon's plane. Finally, a search plane was sent in the direction of the drop zone, and it didn't take long for the crew to find it.

Billows of smoke could be seen from miles away. By the time they arrived, fire had consumed all but the wing tips and tail section of the plane.

The Missing Air Crew report included this statement from the pilot of the search plane:

> *We found it crashed and burning about two hundred yards below this target... Survey from the air indicated that engine or propeller failure caused a forced landing in the wash just under the target, which is characterized by particularly vicious down drafts. Replies to our dropped messages indicated there were no survivors...*

There was also an eyewitness report from an Army Air Forces captain on the ground who was waiting for the supplies:

*Members of this station reached the scene of the crash but could do very little because of intense heat from burning gasoline. Search was made for survivors thrown clear but to no avail. Eight bodies were found in wreckage but none can be identified.*

Then:

*Deceased will be buried at dusk on 30 October 1943 at scene of crash. Report will follow giving location and registration of graves...*

The telegram addressed to Mrs. Nina B. Raff arrived at my grandparents' home on November 9. It said simply:

*The Secretary of War desires me to express his regret that your husband First Lieutenant Lyndon O. Raff has been reported missing in action since Twenty Nine October in Asiatic area. If further details or other information are received you will be promptly notified.*

100

Grandma delivered this devastating news to her daughter in a letter.

∞

"One of the great things about working at Langley," Mom told me some two decades later, "was the vacation time. They gave us one-sixth of a day off every week, beginning the day we started. So by the end of October, Jo and Louise and I had *five* paid vacation days coming to us!"

"What did you do with them?"

Her eyes shone with excitement.

"We decided to go to New York! You know, shop, go to fancy restaurants, see plays, go sightseeing; you name it. So we got our airline tickets, made hotel reservations, and got tickets to three Broadway plays. It was going to be the trip of a lifetime!"

They were set to leave on Saturday, November 13. On Friday night, the three girls left work in high spirits, and during the entire forty-five-minute bus ride home, they chattered away excitedly about what they wanted to buy in New York, which outfits they were bringing, and the sights they most looked forward to seeing.

"But you know," Mom mused, "the minute we got back to the boarding house, I knew something was wrong."

Meeting them at the door, their sour-faced landlady informed them bluntly that she was changing the status of the boarding house to "military use."

And that meant the girls had exactly one week to vacate

the premises—the week they were planning to spend in New York.

"Well," Mom remembered, "we went into a huddle, and it took us about thirty seconds to decide that we were going to New York *anyway,* and we'd figure the rest out later."

Then, giggling with excitement, she and Louise ran upstairs to finish packing, while Jo checked the hall table for the day's mail. After riffling through the stack, she grabbed a few envelopes and followed her friends upstairs.

"Nina!" she called. "You got a letter from your mother!"

She handed her the envelope as casually as if it were a handkerchief, not realizing the devastating news it contained.

∞

There seemed to be no point in sitting around and worrying—it certainly wouldn't solve anything—so they went to New York anyway. Jo and Louise most likely hoped that the sights, sounds, and smells of New York would be exactly what their friend needed, something to distract her and ease her mind. Mom herself was in denial.

"I was sure that the Army was mistaken," she told me. "Maybe someone didn't realize he was on leave for a day or two. Or maybe his plane ran out of gas somewhere in India, and he was already on a bus back to the base. I just *knew* that once I got back from New York, I'd find out everything was fine."

But she went through that week like a sleepwalker, only half-present as she shopped, only half-hearing the lines of dialogue at the theatre, only half-tasting the food.

102

Always at the back of her mind was the nagging question: Where *is* he?

A picture of the three girls taken in a hansom cab in Central Park shows Mom sitting in the middle, smiling faintly, showing no hint of what had to have been churning inside.

Pinned to her jacket, above her heart, were Lyndon's silver pilot's wings.

"I just kept thinking that if I kept wearing them and really believed in their magic, he would come back," she recalled sadly.

After all, hadn't he told her so himself?

**Mom (center) wearing Lyndon's wings**
**Central Park, NY - November 1943**

CHAPTER SEVEN

# Taking a Chance on Love

Mom's luck failed her utterly the minute she got back from New York. Meeting the girls at the front door of the boarding house, their sour-faced landlady told them she had rented their rooms to four young bachelor Army officers. And the officers had already taken up residence. She had stowed all of the girls' belongings in a closet, and they could leave them there for a day or two. But they would have to find someplace else to live, starting that very night.

The four soldiers, who happened to be in the foyer when the girls arrived, were horrified when they heard this pronouncement. They hadn't realized the girls were going to be evicted because of them.

One of them, a handsome dark-haired lieutenant with eyes the color of teak wood, tried to intervene.

"Listen, we'll just move back to the base," he said earnestly to the landlady. "We don't want to kick anybody out!'

She eyed him coldly.

"If you want to do that, it's your business. But these girls were told in advance that they had to be out by now. And I want them out of here in two days at the most. After that, I'll rent the rooms to someone else if you don't want them."

Sighing with relief, Mom turned her attention to the stack of mail on the hall table. That's when she saw that another letter had arrived from her mother—the one telling her that Lyndon had been killed in action.

∞

Okay, it was time to address the elephant in the room. We'd been dancing around all summer, and now I finally had to put it out there.

"So how did he die?" I asked, not daring to look up at her as I took a stitch in the hem of a skirt.

"Plane crash," she said, almost matter-of-factly.

Well, I'd guessed that much. I waited silently for more details.

"They overloaded the plane," she explained, "and it couldn't get off the ground. It ended up cartwheeling down the runway and crashing. All nine guys on board were killed."

"Oh my God! What did you do?"

She stood up, put her sewing aside, and said simply, "Well, there was nothing I *could* do. And now, I need to go make dinner."

I was aghast. Was she just going to end the story on this terrible note and go make dinner?

Before she reached the bedroom door, I leaped off the bed and wrapped myself around her in a bear hug. She was surprised, but soon she relaxed and hugged me back. Poor Mom. Poor Lyndon.

I would hear the rest of the story later on, many times. The following day, from morning until night, the girls pounded the pavement looking for a room, an attic, or any hole in the wall that could offer them shelter. They finally settled on a single room for the three of them. The soldiers insisted on helping them move and hauled endless cartons, trunks, hat boxes, and stacks of clothes to the new room, which was just a few blocks away. Mom did her share too, and was glad to have something distracting to do.

Once the move was completed, they all went out for a meal. It was a congenial group, made closer because it was wartime. All of them were young and far from home, doing things they never imagined, and on their way to God-knows-where. It was nice for everyone to be able to just sit and talk and take a breather. The guys, recent graduates of Officer's Candidate School, were stationed in Virginia for one more week of training. Then, after a short leave, they'd be sent overseas.

Mom remembered that she said very little during the meal but found it comforting to be in the company of men. All four guys knew about her terrible loss and were extremely solicitous. But the dark-haired soldier was particularly wonderful. His name was Jay Taylor, and he made her feel so comfortable that she actually told him a bit about Lyndon and what had happened.

"It was a relief for me to be able to put my feelings into words," she recalled, "even just briefly."

During the week that followed, the little group got together a few more times to eat and talk. And at the end of their last evening together, Jay gave her a piece of paper with his home address written on it. He was leaving for Delaware the next day and didn't know where he was going to end up, but he said lightly, "If you feel like writing, I'd love to hear from you."

She smiled wanly, thinking of the letters she'd written to Lyndon almost daily over the past two years. It was hard to believe she wouldn't be doing that anymore.

**First Lieutenant Jay Taylor, 1945**
**Age 27**

"Sure," she said to the hopeful young soldier who stood before her offering his address. Then she tucked the piece of paper into her purse and promptly forgot about it.

Just three weeks later, Mom was living in Los Angeles. Tired of Virginia, sick of sharing one room with two roommates, and dying to get away from a town wholly dedicated to war, she jumped at the chance when Louise suggested they chuck it all and move to the West Coast. There was a booming aviation industry out there, so they should be able to find jobs. Their friends warned them it was risky, but the girls did it anyway.

They got lucky, finding a furnished three-bedroom Spanish cottage in West Los Angeles for a ridiculously low $100 a month. Both found jobs at North American Aviation, and within a week of arriving, Mom bought her first car (never mind that she'd never driven before). It wasn't long before she was at the wheel, making the twenty-mile trip to and from work every day.

In December, only six weeks after Lyndon's death, Mom actually sat down and wrote Christmas cards, and it was while addressing envelopes that she stumbled upon Jay Taylor's address tucked into her address book. Without thinking too much about it, she dashed off a quick note telling him she'd wound up in L.A. and giving him her new address. Then she dropped the card into the mailbox and didn't give it another thought.

Life in Los Angeles turned out to be good. North American was quite a genial workplace, and because she enjoyed thinking about those days, I heard about them several times.
"The whole gang at the office socialized together. We took horseback riding lessons and went on weekend fishing trips. We even took flying lessons! I learned how to do loop-de-loops in a

plane—you know, turning up the nose of the plane until you're flying upside down, then bringing the plane right side up again."

Yikes. That seemed like a pretty crazy thing for *anyone* to do, let alone someone who'd just lost her husband in a plane crash. She also threw herself wholeheartedly into the social whirl, going to concerts at the Hollywood Bowl, clubs like the Coconut Grove and the Hollywood Canteen, restaurants like the Brown Derby, and other glamorous places. Because her mathematician job paid very well, she always had plenty of money. "You know," she told me, giggling a little, "sometimes I'd find an old paycheck in my purse that I'd actually forgotten to cash. I had *that* much money!"

With a car, friends, and lots of cash, she was free to do just about whatever she wanted.

But listening to her stories sometimes gave me pause. After all, wasn't she a war widow? Shouldn't she have been holed up in a dark room and crying her eyes out? I didn't ask, but it seemed to me that her reaction to Lyndon's death was simply to shut her mind and forge ahead. When thoughts of Lyndon and dreams of their life together surfaced (and they *must* have, from time to time), she just stuffed them down and plunged headlong into another activity. She confirmed this (at least somewhat) some years later when she told me that the whole idea of Lyndon's death had seemed unreal to her for a very long time.

**Mom (left), Louise, and an unidentified friend**
**Los Angeles, 1944**

"It was like a hallucination or a strange bad dream," she recalled. "The thinking part of my brain kept asking, 'Did it *really* happen?' And I think it's because there wasn't any proof; no rituals, no body to view, nothing visible that could help me get it into my head that he was really gone."

Plus, her life hadn't really changed. If they had been living together and he suddenly died in a car accident, the change would have been immediate and shocking. But at the time of Lyndon's death, Mom was used to living alone. She hadn't seen him in nine long months, during which she'd moved twice and begun a whole new life and career in a place that had nothing to do with him. Thus, when he died, her day-to-day life stayed exactly the same, except for the absence of his letters. So it was easy to block the horror of losing him; to just pretend it never happened—at least some of the time.

However, the past did come calling now and again. In the spring of 1944, about six months after Lyndon's death, the government sent home his beat-up old Army trunk, full of his clothes, boots, and a few other possessions, including the glamour shot of Mom wearing the double strand of pearls.

That is, the trunk was sent to my *grandparents'* house. Grandma signed her daughter's name to the receipt, stowed the trunk in her attic, and told Mom about it in a letter. Then Mom decided to leave the trunk in her parents' attic until she was settled somewhere permanently.

There was also the matter of Lyndon's life insurance.

When months had gone by with no word from the Army, she wrote a letter of inquiry to the Veterans Administration and the reply absolutely floored her. Lyndon's beneficiary, they asserted, was not her. It was his mother, Josephine Raff.

Yet she had a very clear memory of Lyndon telling her he'd changed the beneficiary from his mother to her. Yes, he'd come home shortly before he went overseas and told her that!

So what happened? He couldn't have changed his mind. He would have wanted to provide for his wife, an unemployed student at the time, who could easily have been pregnant. But the VA insisted their paperwork showed his mother as beneficiary.

It was a mystery that would never be solved. Most likely, a clerk forgot to record the change, or the paperwork ended up in the wrong stack. But whatever the reason, Mom would never receive a penny's worth of compensation for her husband's death. The entire $10,000 insurance payout went to his mother.

About the same time, in March 1944, Mom received a letter that made her catch her breath. It was an Army issue envelope with an overseas postmark. Looking closer, she realized that, no, it was not from Lyndon; it was from someone she'd almost forgotten—Jay Taylor, the soldier she'd met in Virginia.

The letter he wrote was sweet and funny. He said that right after Christmas, just before he shipped out, he had taken one last trip to the post office to check his mail. And he found her Christmas card there, with her new address. If he hadn't checked his mail that one last time (and he almost didn't), he would have

113

missed it. Now, almost three months later, he was settled into his new assignment supervising a ship repair facility in New Guinea, and finally had the time to write. His letter was cute, she thought, but she put it aside and never got around to replying.

A month went by before another letter arrived from Jay. The envelope contained four pieces of writing paper, each bearing one word: "OKAY" "DAMMIT" "DON'T" "WRITE!"

Now *that* made her laugh. She sat down and dashed off a note to him immediately. Thus began a two-year courtship conducted solely through letters that would radically change both their lives.

∞

An epic year in American history, 1945 was marked by fierce national pride, joy approaching mania, and everywhere, *everywhere*, a huge, collective sigh of relief. World War II was finally over, and the Allies were victorious!

Because the war was so all-encompassing, it actually had two endings: one in Europe on May 8 and one in Japan on August 15. But it was the latter that signaled the culmination of the world's longest and most horrendous nightmare.

Everyone who lived to see that day would remember for the rest of their lives where they were and what they were doing when they heard the glorious news. Mom was in Yosemite National Park, camping with girlfriends, when news broke of the Japanese surrender.

"I was standing there, stirring a pot of stew over an old

camp stove," she recalled, "when suddenly this middle-aged man came barreling through the campground shouting, 'It's over! It's over!' at the top of his lungs. Well, I thought he had to be crazy. What's over?"

Then he bellowed, "The Japs have surrendered! The war is OVER!"

The spoon she was using slipped from her hand, clattered down the side of the camp stove, and landed in the dirt.

"I could hardly breathe. I just kept wondering, could it really be true?"

As if on cue, campers suddenly began pouring out of their tents and cabins, curious about the commotion. And when the news sank in, suddenly all boundaries between strangers vanished. People who had barely looked at each other just a minute before were suddenly throwing their arms around each other, cheering, laughing, and crying.

"We won! We won!" screamed a small boy as he flew by on his bike. "The war is over!"

"God bless America!" an elderly woman called out, her eyes heavenward and her hand over her heart.

"Oh, my gosh, I can't believe it's finally over!" squealed a young girl. "Now the boys can come home!"

"Then people just seemed to be drawn together by an invisible magnet into one big joyful crowd," Mom said. "And I got swept into the middle of it, laughing, cheering and hugging people I'd never seen before. It was incredible—a one-of-a-kind experience. We'd finally made it through the war!"

But what an appalling price they paid.

Worldwide, fifty to seventy million people had lost their lives. The Soviet Union took the biggest hit, losing some twenty million people—half military and half civilians. The U.S., by contrast, was lucky, losing approximately four hundred thousand military and very few civilians. But to those like Mom, who had paid the excruciating price of losing a loved one, the death toll was at least one too many.

By December the G.I.s were coming home in droves, and First Lieutenant Jay Taylor was among them. He had spent nearly two years in the South Pacific in New Guinea and the Philippines where he was in charge of the maintenance and repair of U.S. ships and marine equipment. The job carried plenty of responsibility; he supervised the hiring, training, feeding, and transporting of some three thousand local natives who served as shipyard employees.

When he arrived in 1944, the shipyards in both New Guinea and the Philippines were plagued by rampant, devastating pilfering. But in both areas, Jay devised an effective new accounting system that seemed to keep the problem in check. It was a big victory for him—the biggest of his young life—he found out that he relished being in charge.

Jay also saw his share of action, doing battle in the New Guinea, Southern Philippines, and Luzon campaigns and participating in the liberation of the Philippines and the Battle of

Leyte Gulf. Pictures of him show a young guy who radiates self-assurance and masculinity. He was finally developing a sense of who he was and what he could accomplish, and his confidence and self-esteem was growing daily by leaps and bounds.

He spent two full years as a soldier in the South Pacific, and forever after would insist that the Army was the best thing that ever happened to him.

**Jay in front of his foxhole**
**Leyte, Philippines – 1944**

On December 15, 1945, four months after Japan surrendered, Jay was one of the hundreds of U.S. soldiers crowding the decks of a massive warship that sailed proudly into the port of Los Angeles, at San Pedro.

117

A roar erupted from the dock as flag-waving friends and family cheered their hearts out for their boys, and a band burst into "God Bless America." Fresh from their magnificent victory in the South Pacific, the heroes were home at last!

As they bounded down the ship's gangplank, duffle bags slung over their shoulders, the ecstatic young soldiers either waved and grinned broadly at the crowd or struggled to look cool and composed. But every last one was searching intently for that special someone.

On the dock, joy and pandemonium reigned: girls bounced up and down, waving wildly and screaming their boyfriends' names; lovers flew into each other's arms; parents bear-hugged their sons and dissolved into tears, and children leaped and shrieked with excitement.

In the middle of this frenetic crowd, a lone young woman, dressed in a smart blue suit and peep-toe heels, stood waiting with butterflies in her stomach. As she watched the soldiers disembark, she hoped she would be able to recognize hers. Even though they'd been corresponding for almost two years and their relationship had taken a serious turn, he was still a stranger in many ways.

Suddenly, she spotted him, and her heart leaped a little: yes, that was him, coming down the gangplank! He had a healthy tan and a lean, muscular body, the product of two years of hard physical work and a diet based on C-rations. Both had made him even more handsome than she remembered.

As she watched his eyes scan the crowd, she suddenly wondered if he might have trouble recognizing *her*! So, she fixed her gaze firmly on his face and waved energetically, hoping he would notice her. And when he finally did, the broad smile that lit up his face radiated happiness and relief.

They came together a little shyly—not surprising since they had never even held hands—then fell into a heartfelt hug. With everyone around them planting big wet kisses on each other, it must have been a bit awkward. But a warm hug and a little peck on the cheek would have to do for now.

For some months Jay had been hinting in his letters about the possibility of the two of them establishing a "meaningful relationship" once he got back to the States. But since the two had never spent any time together, they really needed to get to know each other better before making such a momentous decision.

Unfortunately, Jay was due back in Delaware in just a few weeks to muster out of the service and reclaim his old job at DuPont. Ever the dreamer, he was hoping that spending those weeks with her would solidify their relationship. She was dubious, and even alarmed, but that didn't mean she wasn't interested in seeing how things transpired.

So Jay checked into a cheap hotel in downtown Los Angeles, and the two agreed to see each other every night until he had to leave. At that point, they would reassess their situation and figure out what to do next—if anything.

It was a strange, extremely intense courtship. Their

nightly dates had a resolute, dogged quality to them, even when they weren't actively discussing their future. The pressure, mostly unspoken, was ever-present. They went to dinner, took evening walks, visited the occasional bar or club, and sat on her living room couch talking until the wee hours.

But at the end of two weeks, neither of them felt they'd spent enough time together to make a decision. So, Jay regretfully said goodbye and went back to Delaware to muster out, promising to return.

She was skeptical. "People say a lot of things," she told me decades later, waving her hand dismissively. "I was pretty sure it was the last I'd ever see of him."

But he did come back, and they picked up where they had left off, with nightly dates and long weekends together until, finally, it was do-or-die time. Either they were getting married, or Jay was going back to Delaware for good.

They decided to take the plunge.

"It was like holding hands, jumping off a cliff, and hoping we'd survive the fall," she remembered. "We had no idea how it would work out. All we knew was that we didn't want to let each other go."

It was a true postwar hurry-up wedding, planned in a month's time. They booked the church, ordered a wedding cake from the Farmer's Market bakery (surrendering ten sugar coupons in the process), and rented dishes and silverware.

Somebody gave them a recipe for "Artillery Punch," a fruity drink made with five kinds of liquor that was guaranteed to knock out any guest brave enough to down a few cups. They both had a good laugh over the name, agreeing it was the perfect punch for a postwar wedding.

Then, Mom went to Saks and bought herself a chic pearl grey suit plus some pale pink accessories, while Jay purchased a new double-breasted black suit.

The brief ceremony, attended by forty guests, took place on the afternoon of March 16, 1946. It was a "friends only" kind of affair, since nobody in the family had the money to hightail it out to California so soon after the end of the war. Naturally, all of the friends were Mom's, since she was the one who lived in the area, with the exception of Bob, Jay's roommate at the hotel. After the newlyweds had run down the church steps through a hail of rice, the guests ambled over to the bride's apartment for a cake and punch reception. But Jay, shaken by the importance of the occasion, convinced his new bride to make a pit stop at a local bar for a little fortification before facing the party.

They ended up staying longer than expected, and by the time they reached the apartment, the guests were so bombed on Artillery Punch that some of them had started opening the wedding presents. Even worse, at some point during the evening, someone sneaked into the bedroom and robbed the purses of the female guests. All signs pointed to Bob, although he was never confronted. It was an inauspicious beginning.

**Wedding Day—Mr. & Mrs. Jay Taylor**
**March 16, 1946**

Just four days later, the newlyweds stuffed their car with clothes and wedding presents and hit the road, bound for Delaware. It was the third time in less than four years that Mom had moved to the East Coast: once with Lyndon, once for the Langley job, and now here she was, headed there again with a new husband. Maybe this time it would stick.

One thing was certain: she wouldn't be working as a mathematician in Delaware—there weren't any jobs like that where they'd be living. But that was okay—she was newly married, on an adventure with her new husband, and headed for a new life! As she said many times in later years, "Once the war was over, everyone just wanted to get on with their lives. We'd spent four long years on hold, and we were anxious to get back to the business of *living*!"

Getting married seemed like a fast-track to doing just that, and my parents weren't alone in this thinking: 2.3 million U.S. couples got married in 1946, or 16 out of every 1,000 people (of all ages) in the country.

In search of their own little piece of the rainbow, couples everywhere were taking a chance on love.

∞

My father, Jehu (pronounced Jay-you) Swithin Taylor, born on March 10, 1918 on a farm in Stanton, Delaware, began his life in circumstances that were far from ideal.

His mother, a nineteen-year-old farm girl named Sara Taylor, was the youngest daughter of aging parents who probably regarded her as their "surprise child." Sara's nearest sibling was six years older than her; the eldest, twenty-two years older.

Because Sara's parents were overly indulgent and probably just too tired to rein her in, she grew up to be a rather spoiled, headstrong girl, given to wild ways. And in 1917 the teenage Sara became pregnant out of wedlock. Only two things are known about the father: his last name was Hughes, and he did *not* marry Sara.

Family lore holds that Sara and her mother, Frances, spent the last several months of the pregnancy hiding inside the house, and that when the child was born, Frances pretended the baby was hers. (Never mind that she was sixty-one years old at the time.) The baby's birth was never registered, and "Buddy," as the family called him, was raised on the farm by his grandparents, whom he believed were his parents.

When Buddy was seven years old, he was allowed to choose his formal name. He decided he wanted to be named after his Uncle Jay (the first Jehu Swithin Taylor), and his wish was granted. Happily, during the first eight years of his life, little Buddy/Jay was well loved and cared for by his grandparents. But then tragedy struck: within a week's time, both of his grandparents died suddenly of natural causes.

Sara, whom Jay had always thought of as his sister, suddenly swooped in, packed his things, and informed him that she was his real mother. Then she hauled him back to her house in town, where she was living with her husband, Sherman

Thomas, and their two young sons, a toddler, and an infant.

Neither Sara nor Sherman had ever imagined that one day they would be raising her eight-year-old "mistake." And now that fate offered them no choice, they both resented the situation. Jay, for his part, couldn't understand why he was suddenly living with his sister, or mother, or whoever she was. So, he ran away several times, with the goal of getting back to the farm where he belonged. But each time, he was caught, beaten, and dragged back to town; the mean-tempered Sara refused to put up with any of his nonsense. Jay would later remember his mother brandishing a red-hot poker as she chased him through a field. And there was absolutely no doubt in his mind that she intended to use it.

Sara and Sherman were a pretty wild pair who drank heavily, brawled often, and didn't like to work. Sherman, who long claimed he had a bad back, was chronically unemployed, ensuring that money (or the lack of it) was always a problem. But this didn't stop the couple from adding more children to their family. A girl arrived when Jay was ten, then another boy two years later, increasing both the debt and the chaos in the Thomas family.

Soon, things got so bad that Sara and Sherman forced fourteen-year-old Jay to drop out of school and go to work in a coal mine to support the family. Like a character in a Dickens novel, Jay hauled 100 lb. sacks of coal during the day and went home to his drunken, disparaging "parents" at night.

By the age of fifteen, Jay decided he'd had enough of this crazy, abusive situation, so he went to his Aunt Florence, Sara's much older sister, with a proposal. If she would let him live with her family, he would pay for his own room and board. Aunt Florence was all too familiar with Sara's appalling lifestyle, so she agreed to the deal, providing Jay with a merciful and permanent escape from the Thomas household. He immediately went back to high school and got himself a part-time job to pay the rent.

Not long after Jay moved in with Aunt Florence, he witnessed a vicious drunken fight between Sara and Sherman that made him fear for the future of his five-year-old half-sister, Frannie. Shaken, he went to Aunt Florence and vowed that he would pay for Frannie's room and board as well if she would take her in.

Thus, five-year-old Frannie was able to move into a calm, quiet, well-ordered home, where she lived until she finished high school, Jay paying her way throughout. Frannie, a true success story, eventually won a full scholarship to college and enjoyed a long, successful career as an elementary school teacher.

In early 1941 twenty-two-year-old Jay was finally starting to feel pretty good about his life. He had a decent job as a research lab assistant at the DuPont Co., had purchased his first car, and was finally leading an independent life. And then, suddenly, it all came crashing down. On February 19, a "Notice of Selection" arrived from the U.S. government, making Jay one of the first U.S. soldiers to be drafted for World War II.

By March 3, almost before he knew what hit him, he'd been inducted into the Army as a private and sent to Ft. Sill,

Oklahoma, as part of the 70ᵗʰ Field Artillery Battalion. It was still so early in the war that modern equipment and uniforms hadn't been produced, which meant Jay's unit had to use horse-drawn caissons, and the soldiers wore uniforms left over from World War I, including wrapped leggings and wide-brimmed hats like the Royal Canadian Mounted Police.

Jay belonged to a "horse unit," although his time as a mounted soldier was destined to be brief. After just four months, he fell off his horse, got his foot caught in the stirrup, and was dragged, wrenching his knee severely enough to warrant an honorable discharge from the Army on July 28. The U.S. hadn't even entered World War II yet, and Jay had already served his time and gone back to Delaware.

It wouldn't last long. Once Japan bombed the holy hell out of Pearl Harbor in December, Jay, like just about every other young man at that time, was burning to get into the service and defend his country. Although his knee was still injured, he lied to the medical examiner, saying it was completely healed, and re-enlisted. On September 3, 1942, he was called to active duty.

This time around, however, things would be different. Before, Jay had been a lowly private; now, he was determined to become an officer. As an officer and a gentleman, he believed he could shed his old identity as an unwanted, fatherless boy, used and abused by his family. At long last, he would arrive; he would finally *be* somebody. He eagerly applied for Officer's Candidate School, jumped through every hoop, and was thrilled when he

127

qualified for OCS in the Transportation Corps. He enthusiastically seized this big opportunity, vowing to be the best student and soldier he could possibly be.

His gargantuan efforts paid off. Jay made it through OCS at the top of his class, graduating on October 20, 1943 and receiving his commission as a 2nd lieutenant.

Just a week later, he was sent to Virginia for a four-week training course before going overseas. And there, in the entryway of a rickety old boardinghouse, he met Nina Raff.

In May 1946, two months after their wedding, just about the time Mom finished making curtains for their tiny rented house in Wilmington, she received a letter from the Army. It had been two and a half years since Lyndon's death, and the Army was finally getting around to informing her he had been interred at a U.S. military cemetery in India. The War Department, the letter said, should soon "receive authority to comply, at Government expense, with your wishes regarding final interment, here or abroad, of the remains of your husband."

There was nothing for her to do and no decisions to be made. So, she read the letter twice, folded it carefully, and concealed it under a stack of lingerie in her top dresser drawer. There seemed to be no point in mentioning it to her brand-new husband.

Delaware was just about the worst place in the world for Dad. As a former officer in the Army charged with plenty of responsibility, who had several well-earned successes under his belt, he'd begun to believe he was as good as, or even better than, the next guy. But once he came back to Delaware, he was at the bottom of the heap again.

The first slap in the face came from the DuPont Company, his employer. Some jerk in the personnel department coolly informed him that his old position as a lab assistant was no longer vacant, and the only thing still available was a job raking leaves. When Dad point-blank refused and made a big stink about it, the powers-that-be finally offered him a space in a training program for purchasing agents. Well, it beat raking leaves.

Within a year's time, Dad had earned seven raises, although the pay was still low. And Mom, unfortunately, didn't even have a job. It was a hell of a way to start a marriage: no money, no status, and no real chance of attaining success. To make matters worse, the Delawareans Mom and Dad came in contact with were an unwelcoming bunch. And for Dad, being back in his hometown brought back too many bad memories.

Thus, just over a year after they arrived in Delaware, my parents packed up and headed back to southern California, where the people were friendly, and the rents were cheap. Once there, Mom immediately reclaimed her job at North American, and Dad got a job managing a Shell gas station. It was a promising start— and they were finally living in a place where they both felt good.

129

They spent the next few years just trying to get their feet on the ground. Thanks to a massive postwar influx of people, the southern California housing industry was booming. Seizing an opportunity, Dad enrolled in a training program at Bank of America for real estate appraisers, who were in short supply.

Mom continued to bring in a solid paycheck from North American, and in 1948, with the help of the G.I. Bill, she and Dad joined the ranks of Southern California homeowners. This opened up another moneymaking opportunity for them. After adding landscaping to a new house, they could resell it for a small profit, and use the extra money to buy a slightly more expensive house, that also needed landscaping.

They did this several times, moving from house to house and accumulating a decent bit of cash along the way.

As for their marriage, it's not clear how much of Dad's difficult past Mom knew about before she married him, but she certainly learned about it during those early years. She also found out he had a "short fuse," was prone to explosive anger, especially when he'd been drinking, and liked to drink on a nightly basis.

Another thing she learned in short order was that her new husband didn't want to hear about her first husband. Although it was natural for her to make occasional references to Lyndon and the things they'd done (after all, they were together for four years), Dad bristled whenever she mentioned his name.

130

**Mom at work at North American, 1948**

"You know," he said testily one day, "I can fight a real man. But I can't fight a *ghost.*"

Well, that shut her up.

From then on, she simply stopped talking about Lyndon. That was the main reason she hid the letter from the Army that revealed his place of burial in India.

But when a second letter from the Army arrived in March 1948, nearly two years after the first, she decided to share its news with Dad. The letter said that because it was impossible to identify

131

Lyndon's remains individually, they would be returned to the United States and buried as part of a group in a few months.

Although the first letter had promised that *she* could choose Lyndon's final resting place, this one stated the place of burial would be Fort McPherson National Cemetery in Maxwell, Nebraska, and said she would be informed about the arrangements "in due course." In fact it would take almost another two years before Lyndon's remains actually made it to Nebraska.

Mom knew from the start that attending Lyndon's funeral, whenever it might be, was out of the question. Not only would it cost far too much money, but she'd also have to take time off from work, and secure the blessings of her jealous husband.

However, there was another option. The Army held ceremonies for deceased soldiers regularly at March Air Force Base, which was only about an hour from Los Angeles. The letter telling her about this said the service wouldn't be dedicated to Lyndon alone—several soldiers would be honored. But at least it was *something*.

Mom decided she wanted to go—that she *would* go, even if she went by herself. So, taking a deep breath, she handed the letter to Dad and told him this was something she had to do.

Surprisingly, Dad was quite supportive. Although he didn't want to "fight a ghost," he was apparently in favor of honoring a fallen soldier. Not only did he agree, he also drove her to March Air Force Base and stood by her side throughout the entire ceremony.

There was a wonderful black and white picture taken of her that day (which, sadly, has been lost) showing her dressed in a fur coat and fancy hat, stoically receiving a folded flag presented by an Air Force officer. By then, over four years had passed since Lyndon's death. But it wasn't until that moment that Mom had the opportunity to acknowledge what had happened, and formally say goodbye to her husband.

For her, it was the end of an era; one marked by the giddiness of first love, the thrill of getting married, the privations of war, the pain of separation, and the agony of losing the person she loved above all others.

Now it all officially belonged to the past, and she wouldn't speak of Lyndon for many years. But he would always live secretly in her heart.

Clutching the flag as a lone trumpeter mournfully sounded taps, she looked up at the cloudless blue sky and wondered where in the world her young husband had gone. Wherever he was, she wished him well.

Then, turning, she linked arms with Dad and strode resolutely back into her new life.

∞

Nineteen forty-nine would forever hold a special place in the hearts of my parents because it was the year they welcomed their baby girl, Dawn Annette. Little Dawn was beautiful, Dad was now a full-fledged appraiser for Bank of America, and Mom was about to return to North American after a short maternity leave.

The happy ending they had long hoped for seemed to have become a reality.

**Jay and Nina Taylor, ca. 1949**

134

## CHAPTER EIGHT

# Free-Falling

In generations past, getting married was supposed to be the culmination of every woman's dreams—the beginning of a lifetime of happiness, a "license" to have a baby, and undeniable proof that she was so attractive, desirable, and special that some man was willing to forsake all others just to be with her.

This ideal reached its zenith during the years immediately following World War II, and my mother was certainly swept up in the romance of it. She married twice in less than three and a half years. But what she couldn't have known when the champagne glasses were clinking and the rice was flying over her head was that her second marriage would consume her life, strip her of power, and, for at least a couple of decades, turn her into a shell of her former self.

Things might have been different if Mom could have continued her career after she had a baby. This was the original idea, made feasible by the nice lady next door who was willing to take care of little Dawn for a reasonable fee. In the morning Mom would pass the baby over the fence to the neighbor and hurry off to work at North American. Then in the evening, the baby would be passed over the fence once again into Mom's loving arms.

The plan probably looked good on paper, but what Mom hadn't realized was just how agonizing it was to tear herself away from her baby every morning. And it only got worse when Dawn started getting sick a lot. Although Mom knew her hefty paycheck was necessary to keep the family going, having to pass a sick, crying baby over the fence and race off to work was absolute torture for her. Then one night Dawn started screaming when she was handed *back* to Mom, and that was the straw that broke the camel's back.

Horrified by the thought that her own daughter didn't even know her, Mom had a serious discussion with Dad that night. And the very next day, determined to raise her child herself no matter what the cost, she gave notice at work.

This new arrangement was better for Mom in many ways, and certainly better for the baby, but it would exact a high price from both of my parents. Dad would suddenly find himself under tremendous pressure to perform financially. And Mom would see her power in the marriage and as a person evaporate into thin air. Overnight, she would morph from being a major breadwinner to a dependent housewife stuck at home without a car, taking care of a baby, and doing the household chores. And this new status was really set in stone when I arrived in 1953.

Of course, Mom's situation was far from unique: once the men came home from the war, most married women faced sudden role reversals, increased pressure to conform, and a loss of freedom and power. Even if they had done a man's work with a high degree of skill and competency while the war was raging, during the postwar era, they were expected to go back to the roles of housewife and helpmate willingly, even joyfully, and let the men rule once again. But in Mom's case, it was even worse. She took on the additional role of live-in secretary because Dad had decided to go into business for himself.

After getting a few years' worth of experience under his belt as a real estate appraiser, Dad quit the Bank of America, set up an office in one of our bedrooms, and drafted Mom as his secretary. Her duties included typing his reports, answering our home phone with a cheery "Mr. Taylor's office," and doing the taxes. Dad wore the rest of the hats: salesperson, data collector, evaluator, copywriter, quality control person, and troubleshooter, just to name a few. Although he occasionally went out to meet clients or evaluate properties, most of the time, he was at home writing reports or drumming up clients on the phone. And that meant Mom had very little time to herself. While most housewives had at least a few hours during the day to themselves, Mom's husband was right there in the next room.

And Dad was no easy boss. Impatient, demanding, and controlling, he wanted everything done *now*, no matter what time of the day or night. He liked to start work very early in the morning and sometimes woke Mom up at 5:00 a.m. to type one of his reports. He also insisted that she answer the phone during business hours, even when he could have easily picked up a call himself. This meant she was essentially housebound.

It must have come as a shock, after years of being a valuable part of an aeronautics team, that she was now the invisible support system in Dad's business. And while she didn't complain about her roles, her mood became noticeably darker and more irritable, especially during the three years we lived in an apartment because of a sudden downturn in business.

In 1961 Mom's frustration and dissatisfaction deepened when we moved to Tujunga (pronounced Tuh-hung-gah), a small community nestled in the foothills of the San Fernando Valley, about twenty miles north of downtown Los Angeles. Mom always said that Tujunga was "out in the sticks," and it *was* pretty far off the beaten path. But that made property cheap, and Dad, with his nose for good real estate, found a house for us there. It was in bad shape, but it had "good bones" and was in a nice neighborhood. And it was on the market for $10,000.

Dad didn't bother to ask Mom before racing headlong into the deal. That night, he announced, "Guess what? I bought a house today!"

Mom looked at him for a long moment before replying sarcastically, "Great! Are you going to tell me where it is?"

It was clear where the power lay in their marriage.

Our neighborhood, a tract of 1950s ranch-style houses set on large lots, was cozy, friendly, and teeming with children. Because we lived on a cul-de-sac, there was hardly any traffic, and the neighborhood kids played baseball and kickball in the street without interruption. During this era of stay-at-home moms, we kids ran freely in and out of the neighbors' homes, gobbling homemade cookies and playing with each other's toys under the watchful and loving eyes of our mothers. No daycare or after school programs for us! It was a great place for kids to grow up.

But it wasn't so great for Mom. Tujunga was isolated and had nothing much to offer an intellectually starved, culturally deprived woman like her. The nearest city, Glendale, was about twenty minutes away by car, but our one car belonged solely to Dad, who reserved it for himself in case he might need to run off and look at a property. And Mom couldn't have used the car anyway—she had to be available to answer that damned phone. This pretty much precluded joining clubs, volunteering, or doing anything else requiring time away from home.

To fill up the long hours, Mom read whatever she could get her hands on, powering through sets of literary classics that included works like *"A Tale of Two Cities," "David Copperfield,"* and *"Pride and Prejudice."* She ordered some of the Time-Life book sets and pored over *"The Cell," "The Mind,"* and *"Man and Space."*

She bought herself a two-volume *Encyclopedia of Food Science and Technology* so she could study the chemistry of yeast bread and learn the reasons her cakes fell flat; then she performed experiments in the kitchen. And she spent endless hours at the sewing machine, just like her mother, creating entire wardrobes for Dawn and me, making new cushion covers for our furniture, and even constructing full-length drapes. You name it, she could figure out how to make it; and she did.

Mom's most enjoyable and ongoing project, though, was being a mother. A born teacher, she was always happy to help

Dawn and me with our homework. She liked board games with an intellectual bent and taught us to play Monopoly and Pit, always as a friendly, non-competitive competitor. She started a Camp Fire Girls troop for my friends and me and threw herself enthusiastically into the role of leader. She loved the outdoors and always packed a mean picnic basket to take along on our many jaunts to the local mountains.

Her parenting style could be summed up in one word—*practical*—which is not at all surprising for a girl who came from farm stock and lived through the Great Depression. Her greatest wish for Dawn and me was that we would grow up to be educated, independent women, able to take care of ourselves under any circumstances.

"You can't expect to marry someone rich, or even that you'll marry at all," she often told us. "You've got to be ready to handle whatever comes along, all by yourself. Then, if you happen to be lucky enough to have someone to help you, all the better. But if not, you'll still be okay."

A college education was an absolute must. More than once, her trusty math background had been her ticket to a better life, and Mom wanted the same thing for us. Get yourself something that will guarantee you a job, Mom counseled.

She also made sure we mastered everyday practicalities: things like how to make your own clothes, wax a floor by hand, use correct grammar, wash windows using vinegar and newspapers, behave properly in all situations, sleep with a headful of plastic rollers, and make an effective (though hideous-looking) face masque from Fuller's earth.

And, like any good mom, she provided us with helpful guidelines for getting through life:

"Stand on your own two feet."

"Don't sell yourself short."

"When you have a problem that needs solving, tell everyone you know. Somebody will have a solution."

"Don't open bobby pins with your teeth; you'll chip them."

And especially for my easily riled sister, "Just let it go— like water off a duck's back."

She was the person we turned to whenever we needed anything or wanted someone to explain the world to us. We went to her when we were happy, sad, confused, afraid, elated, annoyed, or in need of validation and love. And we certainly went to her with our math homework! In all things and at all times, she was our rock. And we loved her more than anything.

In 1963, all of my parents' hard work finally began to bear fruit when Dad's earning power as an appraiser reached new heights. By then, his paydays had become so frequent and substantial that he felt ready to pursue a bold, even audacious goal: that of becoming a real estate developer. And he knew exactly where he wanted to start: Newhall, an independent, unincorporated town about forty miles north of downtown Los Angeles, in what is now known as the Santa Clarita Valley.

Newhall, with its undeveloped desert lands dotted with tumbleweeds and gently rolling hills, looked like it had been lifted straight out of the Wild West. But to Dad, it was the perfect site for a major housing development. For one thing, the land was cheap; you could build three houses in Newhall for the price of one in Los Angeles. And that's exactly what he did. He bought three lots and built one house on each of them. Once these homes were sold, he planned to use the profits to build twice that many. And then, who knew? It just might be the start of a huge and profitable new venture.

It sounded like a great idea. Dad drew up the blueprints based on our own house, and Mom helped refine them with practical suggestions to increase their livability. In 1965, Dad located three land parcels up in the hills with spectacular views and no neighbors, and plunked down just about everything he and Mom had. Then, when the bulldozers began leveling the lots early in the summer, Dad got so excited he could hardly stay away. In the evenings, while it was still light, he often piled all of us into the car and drove out to Newhall to check out the progress. And it wasn't long before the houses sprang up, seemingly by magic. Beautiful, airy, and full of modern conveniences, they were homes that anyone would be proud to call their own.

And then the nightmare began. Because the houses were isolated, most buyers and real estate agents weren't even aware they existed, so they sat vacant for a long time. Vandals regularly ripped out garbage disposals, dishwashers, and anything else they could get their hands on, all of which had to be replaced, sometimes repeatedly. Expenses multiplied, but still no sales were made. Dad felt sure it was only a matter of time before the houses sold; we just needed to hang on financially. But the houses didn't sell.

Finally, they had to be rented to tenants who damaged and neglected them and refused to water the yards, which fried under the hot Newhall sun. The chunk of investment money that should have doubled by then was rapidly running down the drain. And so it went, for more than a year of unbearable stress and intense disappointment, until Dad got the worst possible news. The bank was foreclosing on the houses. And we were broke.

Beginning in 1965, and for the next three years, Dad lived in a perpetual state of fury. He'd always been a drinker, but now he ramped up his alcohol intake and started much earlier in the day. Soon, he was cracking his first can of stout malt liquor before breakfast and kept at it throughout the day. By about 4:00 p.m., he started on the hard stuff, usually vodka, and could easily knock off an entire fifth in an evening.

Dad was constantly looking to vent his rage, and any excuse would do—somebody left her shoes out; somebody didn't jump fast enough when he called; somebody forgot to put a folded napkin under his fork before he sat down to dinner, and so on.

His angry explosions became a nightly occurrence at our dinner table. He'd look for the smallest thing to get mad about, fly into a rage, then get up, slam his chair against the wall, and storm off into another part of the house.

Sometimes, he'd come reeling back to the kitchen where we ate our meals and open the cupboard doors, just so he could slam them loudly while swearing under his breath. Other times he'd leave the table, stomp off into the next room, and fall onto the couch. There he'd lie, eavesdropping on our dinner conversation and making snide remarks in a loud voice.

Dad's nickname in Officer's Candidate School had been "Little Caesar," and we came to know that character well over the years, especially during and after Newhall. Little Caesar was always spoiling for a fight. Little Caesar liked to grab his daughters angrily by the arm and shove them up against a wall to make his point. Little Caesar wore heavy wingtip shoes and kicked our dog in the rear when Bud was reluctant to trot outside at night to take a last pee. Little Caesar liked to chain-smoke Camel cigarettes in the car with the windows rolled up. And if Dawn or I cracked open a backseat window to try to get a breath of fresh air, he furiously rolled his window down all the way, blowing us to smithereens as he yelled, "Is *that* what you want?"

And yet, there was another, very different person who lived with us, at least some of the time. His name was Dad. Dad was sweet and sentimental and would wipe away tears when you gave him a mushy birthday card. Dad was the coolest head in the house in an emergency, the one who always knew exactly what to do. Dad was a tender caretaker when we were sick and gave us the best backrubs. Dad told us we were pretty and "the personification of all his dreams." Dad would bring home candy bars and chocolate malts and buy us whatever we wanted if we went to the grocery store with him. If we asked Dad for a dollar, he would always give us two—maybe even more.

Unfortunately, during the Newhall years, Little Caesar was a lot more in evidence than Dad was.

In December 1964, just as the Newhall investment was beginning to fall apart, Grandma died unexpectedly at the age of seventy. Grandpa was shocked to the core—he and everyone else had always expected her to outlive him. Grandpa had suffered a couple of strokes in the 1950s that left him somewhat slower mentally and with a noticeable palsy in his hands, but since Grandma managed the everyday chores and took good care of him, he was fine. Unfortunately, Grandpa, who had never even learned to write a check, was completely unprepared to fend for himself when she died.

He came to our house for an indefinite stay where he was installed in my frilly yellow bedroom while I moved in with Dawn. And then he was expected to make a new life for himself. If Mom felt isolated and bored in Tujunga, it had to have been a million times worse for Grandpa. I remember him sitting at our dinner table shortly after he arrived, crying silently into his soup, while we all watched. Nobody said a word. He had absolutely nothing to do, nowhere to go and no way to get around, other than his own two feet. But the worst part was he had to contend with a bully of a son-in-law who was nice to him in the beginning, but became increasingly belligerent as time went on.

In an effort to be helpful and to do something—anything—productive, Grandpa hung our laundry on the clothesline and brought it back into the house once it was dry. He mowed the lawn and trimmed the bushes. He walked the dog every day. He cleaned out the garage and got rid of excess junk, including a huge wad of tar paper that Dad had stowed out back. But sometimes his well-meaning help didn't pan out too well.

When Grandpa tried to burn that wad of tar paper in our living room fireplace, he almost set the house on fire. When he cleaned out the garage, he accidentally threw out a box of our best Christmas ornaments. And he was always leaving unattended cigarettes around, making burn marks on the furniture. Little Caesar was not at all averse to giving Grandpa the rough side of his tongue when he made these mistakes.

Soon we noticed that Grandpa seemed to be spending an awful lot of time walking the dog, and discovered that he'd found his way to the "Tujunga Brite Spot," a grungy little bar up on Foothill Boulevard where he could drown his sorrows and stay out of the house as long as possible. And who could blame him?

One night I heard my father yelling, and when I crept into the family room to see who was getting it this time, I saw Grandpa standing at the bar separating the den from the kitchen. His back was to me, and Mom and Dad stood on the opposite side.

As I drew closer, I could see that Grandpa was frantically leafing through the pages of a *Life* magazine, while Dad berated him for something he had done. Grandpa was so nervous he couldn't even look at Dad. With his eyes glued to the magazine, he just kept flipping, flipping, flipping the pages as Dad raged on.

The worst part was that Mom stood right next to Dad during this tirade and said absolutely nothing. Little Caesar was going for the jugular, and poor Grandpa was too weak to mount any kind of defense. But Mom just stood there as Dad took her beloved, broken father apart, limb by limb, without offering one word in Grandpa's defense.

A few months later, Grandpa went to stay with Ted and his family and eventually made his way back to Minnesota. He somehow managed to find himself an apartment, and for the first time in his life, he learned to live alone. He shopped, paid the bills, and did all the other chores people have to do if they want to live independently. Not only that; he started going to church every Sunday because, as he said, "It's what Mama would have wanted." The last time we saw Grandpa was when he came to visit us for Christmas in 1968. Just a few months later, on a snowy Sunday morning, he died of a stroke in the foyer of Hamline Church while taking off his overshoes.

Mom always said that once Grandma died, Grandpa was just marking time, waiting to join her. I'm sorry to say that we did nothing to make that time more bearable.

**Mom and Grandpa - Christmas 1968**
**About two months before his death**

The Newhall fiasco set off a pattern of physical intimidation that soon became the name of the game at our house. Dad's favorite way of making us behave was to grab us by the arm and shove us around, sometimes backing us into a corner and yelling into our faces. Once, he grabbed me by my shoulders and thrust me up against a wall so hard that my spine hit the chair rail, and my legs suddenly lost all feeling. It wasn't until I started sliding down the wall that he showed signs of concern.

Another time, when Little Caesar caught me lying, he shoved a bar of soap in my mouth to teach me a lesson. I remember my teeth scraping furrows in the gooey green sides of the bar and brushing my teeth for a long time before I could get the bitter taste of soap out of my mouth. I hated him for that.

Then there was the night when I was lying in bed and Little Caesar kicked my bedroom door open and roared drunkenly, "I'd like to break every bone in your body!"

Evidently, I'd put something down the garbage disposal that had clogged it up.

I lay there quaking, wondering if he was actually going to attack me. In the end, he slammed the door shut and reeled down the hallway, leaving me wide awake and wondering where I could hide if I needed to.

Dawn got it at least as much as I did, and maybe even worse, because she tended to talk back. At one point Little Caesar furiously ripped the front of her blouse, exposing her white bra. She was fifteen at the time. I also remember him tearing at her pajamas, and there was no bra underneath them. Fortunately, the pajamas stayed intact.

While Mom didn't seem to try too hard to stop him from manhandling us, at least she was present during these incidents and didn't leave us to deal with him on our own. And, to be fair, sometimes she did protest from the sidelines. I remember her objecting strenuously to the ripping of perfectly good clothes.

"Jay," she shouted, "Not the clothes! Why rip the *clothes*?"

This struck me as a really odd thing to say. Who cared about ripping the damn clothes? They were a trifle compared to attacking another human being, especially your own daughter. What about the ripping of our *psyches*?

Mom may have been able to stand by and watch him attack us, but I couldn't tolerate it. When Little Caesar turned on Dawn, I always wedged myself between them and screamed, "Leave her alone! Leave her alone!"

As for protecting myself, I came up with a very effective trick. As soon as he lunged for me, I'd drop to the ground and start kicking. My legs were strong from ballet lessons, and I discovered that if I flexed my feet and just kept on kicking, there was no way he could get near me. He'd eventually have to give up and go away. And that, believe it or not, signaled the end of his physical attacks. Once I started doing my drop-and-kick trick, he stopped grabbing me, forever. The psychological abuse, however, would continue.

I have no idea what Mom said to Dad about these drunken incidents—if anything—when they were alone. All I know is that when we were present, she responded to his anger and bad behavior by ignoring him. For example, when Little Caesar started making a scene at our dinner table (his favorite forum), she simply sipped her coffee, continued eating her meal, and made polite conversation with us. The three of us would sit there, with candles flickering and "Stardust" playing dreamily in the background while Little Caesar swore, shoved his chair violently against the wall, and slammed cupboard doors. Then Mom would turn to us and inquire genially, "So, what happened at school today?" It was surreal, to say the least.

If Mom's response to Dad's craziness was to ignore it, Dawn's was to go out with her friends as often as possible. She was sixteen when Newhall fell apart, and she had plenty of friends and dates who would pick her up and sweep her off to another world.

My response was to escape to the ballet studio. Oddly enough, I really hated ballet when I started at age eleven, in 1964. It was Mom's brainy idea. She enrolled me because she hated my posture; like a typical kid, I stood with my stomach sticking out, back swayed and shoulders rounded. Ballet classes, she thought, were the route to an elegant carriage.

The trouble was, ballet hurts. If your back and legs aren't strong and flexible, all that bending and kicking and holding your leg suspended in the air is agonizingly hard work. Plus, you feel and look like a klutz because you can't fake those very precise movements. From the tilt of your head to the tips of your toes, each step must be performed in an exacting and completely unnatural manner. It takes strength, flexibility, endurance, and—most of all—a good understanding of technique. All of these take years to develop. You don't get there overnight.

But I got lucky.

After suffering through ballet classes for about a year, something suddenly clicked, and by 1966, I started to enjoy dancing. Then my teacher invited me to join a small dance troupe, and even though I only had tiny parts in these ballets, I got bitten by the performing bug, big time. All I wanted was to become a better dancer so I could get bigger and better parts.

And yet, there was more to it than that. The world I encountered at the ballet studio was the total opposite of the one I lived in at home. Ballet is truly magical, a make-believe universe based on beauty and fantasy and set to magnificent music. I fell in love with the romance, beauty, and exquisite language of dance, and raced headlong into that world. I wanted to spend my life dancing in Giselle's village or gliding serenely on Swan Lake. It was beautiful—and *so* much better than real life.

Not surprisingly, Dad's business began to slide downhill during Newhall, and then it just kept on going. His alcoholism interfered with his abilities to find new clients, interact with them successfully, and produce high-quality work. And while he did manage to find enough work to keep our little family out of debt, our bank account dwindled to new lows. Mom prayed that it was just a phase; that both Dad and the business would recover.

Unfortunately, neither one did.

Years later, Dad would be proven right about the viability of housing developments in the Santa Clarita Valley. Unfortunately, he was about two decades ahead of his time. For four straight years in the 1980s, Santa Clarita proved to be the fastest-growing region in Los Angeles County. And by 2015, it boasted a population of 230,000. But for Dad (and the rest of us), it all happened far too late.

In 1968, a year that would see the assassinations of Bobby Kennedy and Martin Luther King, Jr., the ramping up of the Vietnam War, and violent protests at the Democratic Convention in Chicago, the turbulence inside our own home continued. Our finances had waned alarmingly, a fact emphatically hammered home whenever I asked for a dollar to buy a pair of nylons.

"We're living on *savings!*" Mom would reply, exasperated. All I knew was I needed some nylons.

With tensions running high, Dad's simmering anger came out in all the standard ways, but he also found a new target for his fury: my ballet teacher.

By then, I was going to ballet class three or four times a week, plus rehearsals, plus the various shows we put on around town. My generous teacher, Miss Rose, who was never in it for the money (dancers never are), offered scholarships to her performing students. We were allowed and encouraged to take all the classes we wanted at her studio for $14 a month. Since a one-hour class typically cost $3.50, this was a great deal for me.

The trouble was neither of my parents was on board with my dancing. As far as Mom was concerned, my ballet classes had served their purpose: my posture problem had disappeared, so the classes could disappear as well. Besides, they cost money. But Dad had a different reason: he was jealous of my teacher.

"You'll do anything *she* says," he stormed, "But you never listen to me."

This, of course, was totally ridiculous. But Dad's animosity toward my ballet lessons continued to grow.

First, there was that ten-minute drive to the studio that both of my parents found intrusive and a pain in the neck.

Then there was the $14 a month fee for unlimited lessons, which Dad thought was too much and began to refuse to pay. Fortunately, I was able to scrape up the money myself by babysitting.

But the straw that broke the camel's back was my being cast as a swan in our dance school's production of *Swan Lake*. As soon as summer vacation started, I would be expected to be at the studio every day for rehearsal for the entire two weeks preceding the show.

Knowing this was going to stir up a hornet's nest at home, I came up with an elaborate charade to fool Dad. Every morning, I hid my dance bag in our neighbor's bushes, announced that I was going to visit them, retrieved my bag, and walked the mile and a half to the studio. After rehearsal, I walked home, stashed the bag, and sauntered through the back door like nothing had happened.

Mom knew what I was doing, but Dad was oblivious. This went on for about a week, until the inevitable day when I didn't have enough time to make the walk. Mom started the car as I hurried out the kitchen door, dance bag in hand.

Suddenly, Little Caesar came to life and bellowed, "Where are you going?"

"Rehearsal," I called over my shoulder, slamming the door behind me.

He came barreling after me.

"You didn't eat your lunch!"

"I did too! I ate a peanut butter sandwich!" By this point, I'd reached the car and yanked the door open.

"You did not! Get back in here and eat your lunch!"

I threw my dance bag into the backseat and jumped in front, but Dad caught up with me before I could shut the door. He grabbed me by the waist and tried to drag me out of the car, roaring, "You get back in here!"

I held on to the hump on the floor of the car and screamed, "I ate! I ate!"

Then Mom finally shouted, "Oh Jay, let her go! She ate her lunch!"

He let me go. I slammed the car door and hunkered down in my seat as Mom backed the car down the driveway.

Once we were finally free of him, she turned to me and sighed.

"You know...we can't go on this way," she said.

I stared out the window, not saying a word, but I knew she was right. Of course, we had to give in. We always did.

Whatever it took to keep Dad happy, we did, no matter how ridiculous or unfair it might be. Trying to fight him just didn't work.

"You'd better tell your teacher you aren't coming to ballet anymore after Swan Lake is over with," she said.

And so, I did. I quit ballet at the beginning of the summer of 1968, then faced three interminable months during which I had nothing to do and nowhere to go—except hideous summer school.

No wonder I was so eager to immerse myself in Mom's stories of love and romance way back in the 1940s.

I pretty much stopped thinking about Mom and Lyndon and their tragic love story once the summer of '68 ended and school started again. It was as if I'd seen a movie that I liked a lot, then stowed it somewhere in the back of my mind. Other things were a lot more pressing, like my crazy class schedule that included five solids and tons of homework, a certain boy that I had a crush on, and plenty of other distractions. Mom and I didn't have much time to sit around and chat anymore.

But the tree incident brought it all back. It happened on a Sunday evening in December of that year. Dawn and I were sitting in front of the TV watching the Ed Sullivan show, with our wet, freshly shampooed hair dripping on towels slung around our shoulders. She was combing the knots out of her hair while I wrapped mine around hard plastic rollers.

A 70 mph wind raged outside, and Dad was drunk and sulking in the bedroom, after throwing a fit about some silly thing. Then suddenly, Mom noticed that a young tree in our front yard was starting to give way. If the wind kept up, our little tree would surely blow over.

She hurried down the hall to tell Dad and we heard his angry voice booming from the other end of the house.

"You're so goddamn smart, *you* fix it!" he yelled.

Dawn and I looked at each other and rolled our eyes. So typical. When Mom came back, the three of us shrugged on our jackets without a word. Then we ventured out into the freezing wind, wet heads and all, to try to save our tree, which had almost blown over a couple of times before.

To help stabilize the tree during high winds, Dad had nailed the end of a chain to the roof. The chain, which could be wrapped around the trunk of the tree and then hooked to its point of origin on the roof, would hold the tree upright.

Mom hauled a ladder out of the garage, climbed up to the edge of the roof, and tossed me the end of the chain.

"Here!" she shouted, her voice barely audible through the wind. "Get the tree straight and wrap this chain around it!"

With our teeth chattering, Dawn and I struggled to shove the tree into an upright position against a fierce wind that blew our jackets open and even snatched a curler out of my hair.

After what seemed like forever, we managed to straighten the tree and wrap the chain around it. Mom pulled on the chain with all her might, trying to hook it to the roof, which took several tries and all of her strength before she was successful. Then, once the tree was finally stabilized, the three of us ran back inside to get warm.

It wasn't the first time this kind of thing had happened. A few months earlier, we'd had a rainstorm, and a big wet spot developed in the ceiling above Dawn's bed. It was the same deal: Dad was mad about something and told us all to shove it. So, Dawn went up into the attic to try to fix things and accidentally put her foot through the wet spot, making a big hole in the ceiling right above her bed. And it stayed that way for a while until we finally got someone in to fix it. Now Dad was making us freeze to death while we tried to shore up that tree.

*He* was the man of the house, I thought angrily as I hung up my jacket and wrapped a towel around my freezing head. *He* should take care of these things. What the hell were we doing in that icy wind, unprotected and struggling with something that took real muscle power, while the man in our lives lay in bed just a few feet away? That wasn't the way a man was supposed to act. Would *Lyndon* be telling us to get lost and figure out our problems by ourselves? Would he be knocking back a fifth of vodka every night and working up a head of steam over nothing? Would Mom be stuck in the role of *his* personal servant? Would he make me quit ballet just because he was jealous of my teacher?

It was the first time I truly realized that we'd been dealt a lousy hand and deserved a lot more. And it was the first time I thought that Mom would have had a better life—maybe even much better—if it weren't for that damned plane crash.

## CHAPTER NINE

# The Reclamation

Fast forward about eighteen months to the spring of 1970. Mom was desperate because the family was going under financially. Dad's business was completely in the toilet, and she knew she had to get some kind of job—anything to pay the bills. But what could she do, stuck in Tujunga with no transportation and a mathematician's resume dating back some twenty years? It was an impossible situation, but *something* had to give.

And then a Great Miracle occurred. On April 13 the teachers in the L.A. Unified School District decided to go on strike. And it was *war*. Their main gripes were typical: lousy pay and low status. But they also wanted smaller classes and more money spent on reading programs. LAUSD teachers had gone on strike a few times in the past, but this time they were deadly serious and in it for the long haul. Over half of them left their jobs and walked the picket lines for five excruciatingly long weeks.

Those weeks weren't a bit excruciating for me, however. As a senior in high school with only two months to go until graduation, I was thrilled to hear that the administration had decided to stop taking attendance for the duration of the strike. I couldn't think of a single reason *not* to cut school. So, on most days, as soon as I was dropped off at school, I hopped into another car with a bunch of friends and headed up into Big Tujunga Canyon, where we hung out at an old swimming hole. Or we went to Taco Bell, the movies, or someone's house to sit around and talk—anything other than going to school. And we weren't alone. At the height of the strike, almost half of the 650,000 students in our district stayed away, even though every single campus stayed open.

Too bad there were still 325,000 diehard kids showing up every day, because they posed a huge problem for the administration. Although the staff was gutted, they still had to keep all those kids in their seats and busy—and maybe even teach them something. But while this may have been a problem for LAUSD, it turned out to be a windfall for Mom, who saw an opportunity in the making. She had a math degree; why couldn't she be a math teacher at our local junior high for the duration of the strike? She made an appointment with the principal, who not only agreed to take her on, but got her an emergency teaching credential, and hustled her into the classroom straightaway.

It would prove to be Mom's first step toward reclaiming her identity, her independence, and her self-esteem.

She must have seemed like a godsend to the administration. Even in the best of times, math teachers were few and far between, but during the strike, they were practically nonexistent. Then, in walks someone who not only understands and loves math but wants to teach it.

Yes, Mom certainly was well-versed in math. But she'd never taught and had only the vaguest notion of what typical 1970s kids were like. The kids she knew from our neighborhood were basically nice and well-behaved. But in the classroom, Mom discovered a whole different breed of teenager, some of whom offered her interesting and shocking insights into the state of modern youth. Suddenly, she was subjected to regular doses of profanity, off-the-wall hyperactivity, rudeness, cheating, sex talk, and blatant disrespect. Some of the teenage boys could be extremely difficult to handle, and on more than one occasion, she was physically threatened. But she always insisted that she preferred the boys to the girls, who could be snotty, cold, and extraordinarily devious.

Way out of her depth and with no classroom experience, Mom forged ahead, struggling to explain positive and negative numbers, the Pythagorean Theorem, and how to figure the circumference of a circle to a bunch of squirrelly students who couldn't care less. Spitballs flew, kids asked deliberately stupid questions, background chatter escalated to a din, and a few deadheads literally slept through class.

Mom's response was to laugh off some of this behavior, send the incorrigibles to the principal, and keep on going. At the end of the day, she dragged herself home totally beat, yet surprisingly exhilarated. After twenty years of being housebound, she was out in the world again, doing something important and earning a much-needed paycheck.

Because math teachers were so few and far between, Mom's temporary strikebreaking job turned into a long-term substitute position, then morphed into a full-fledged teaching job that lasted two decades. At one of the lowest points of her life, she finally found her wings.

Suddenly, basic expenses were covered, and a little bit of money could even be squirreled away for a rainy day. There was no more danger of losing the house or going into debt, and no more worrying about when Dad would land his next job. What a relief!

And lessened anxiety wasn't the only welcome change. Almost overnight, my parents' roles reversed. Mom went out into the world every day, and Dad became the "stay-at-home" who made her breakfast, drove her to school (we still had only one car), and picked her up at 4:00 p.m.—all without being asked. He hauled her bag, books, and papers into the house after school, where he had a snack waiting for her.

Then he sat with her at the kitchen table, puffing on a cigarette while she ate, and listened to her vent about the kids, the administration, the school board, and a million other things that annoyed her. It was a release for her and a welcome diversion for him.

Because it was still early in the afternoon, he usually hadn't started in on the hard liquor yet, so he could concentrate on what she said. Then, once she finished her snack and her diatribe, she collapsed on the couch while Dad made dinner.

Yes, things were certainly different at our house once Mom started teaching.

164

Am I making it sound like Dad got a personality transplant once Mom started teaching? He didn't. These welcome changes were pretty much confined to daytime. Little Caesar still had plenty of anger to unleash at night, when he was usually drunk.

Mom, however, had become less inclined to accept it. One night, Little Caesar spied a pea that had fallen on the floor and ordered Mom to pick it up. She looked at him like he was crazy, pulled herself up tall, and said, "I will not!"

"Pick up that pea!" Dad insisted.

She held her ground and shot back, "I will *not* pick up that pea! *You* pick up that pea!"

Dawn, who by then was living away at college but happened to be home that night, suddenly burst into gales of laughter at the absurdity of the situation. Through some miracle, that broke the tension. Dad actually began to laugh and went back to eating. But Mom had won that round.

There was another time, however, when he wasn't so genial. They were arguing in the kitchen, and for once, she wasn't backing down and taking his guff. Finally, in frustration, he grabbed her by the wrist.

And that's when I saw my mother turn to steel, right before my eyes. She looked him straight in the eye, and said through gritted teeth, "Don't you *dare* manhandle me!"

He backed off immediately. And to my knowledge, he never tried it again.

With Mom a no-go and Dawn away at college, the obvious choice for someone to grind under his heel was me. A very young seventeen-year-old at the time, living at home and going to junior college, I had all the qualifications: no car, no job, and no money. In other words, I was totally dependent on Dad.

That meant he was free to denigrate me, saying things like, "Jeez, you look like a dago," when I showed him my senior picture, or "You look like a tramp," when I put on a mini skirt. When I dared to offer a rare political opinion, if it didn't mirror his own beliefs, he'd shake his head disgustedly and remark, "You know, for a smart girl, you sure say some stupid things."

His favorite battleground, always, was the dinner table, and his favorite topic was my piss-poor knowledge of current events. Because I didn't read the newspaper, listen to news broadcasts, or read news magazines, I was almost completely ignorant about what was going on in the world. Little Caesar knew he could always rant about this, and he'd start by saying something like:

"So, Nadine, what do you think about what's going on in Cambodia?"

I'd fiddle with my napkin and glance out the window, thinking, "Oh brother, here we go again." Too bad turning invisible or flying straight through the glass was never possible.

"I don't know," I'd reply listlessly.

"You don't know?" he'd repeat, as if surprised.

Silence.

"Did you know they're having a civil war there right now?"

"No."

"No. You don't know about that," he'd say in a voice dripping with disdain. Then he'd begin to warm to his real subject, which was what an idiot I was.

"I don't understand you. You have no idea about what's going on in the world around you. You don't read the newspapers, you don't watch the news! Christ, you don't know a stinkin' goddamn thing about anything...!"

He'd continue in this vein while I stared out the window or at my plate or across the room, doing my best to block out his noise and think about something else.

Finally, he'd get himself so worked up that he'd storm out of the kitchen, head for the bedroom, and fall onto the bed, where he'd listen to talk radio until he fell asleep. It was probably only about 7:30 p.m. at this point, but he'd be out for the night.

Mom and I would just look at each other and sigh with relief. Then we'd take up some pleasant topic of conversation and go on as if nothing had happened. Once or twice, she tried to explain that the real reason Dad got mad was he needed an excuse to leave the table. The liquor had killed his appetite, but he didn't want to admit it. I didn't care why he left; I was just glad to see him go.

My table setting skills were also fodder for a rant. He'd scrutinize the table before sitting down, searching for the slightest omission: a missing salad fork, the wrong size serving spoon, the lack of a napkin folded under his fork, or candles that weren't lit. Another sin was the lack of hors d'oeuvres (in his book, this meant a dish of olives or pickles). Obviously, he just wanted something to yell about.

You'd think I would have started reading the newspaper and made sure there were pickles on the table, if only out of self-defense. But I never did. Instead, I ignored him, building thicker and thicker walls around myself, only responding when he made a fuss. The rest of the time, I pretended he didn't exist. If I could have made him disappear, I would have. Instead, I began to disappear.

By the time I started attending our local junior college, the atmosphere at home had grown so oppressive that I felt like there was something wrong inside my head—as if I had some kind of a "cold" mentally, or my brain had been wrapped in cotton. I wandered around the college campus in a fog, dodging my friends and hiding out in the library. I took a personality test in my "Marriage and Family Living" class and scored in the "pathological" sections of "submissiveness" and "hostility." I didn't want to do anything but sleep. I couldn't wait for that golden day when I would go away to college and escape.

Amazingly, it was during this period that I met my first boyfriend. Charlie was in my psychology class, and, for whatever reason, he developed a crush on me from afar. He was cute, he was a football player, and he seemed nice. And when he walked up to me and started a conversation one day, it was the beginning of a year-long romance that made me feel like I was a human being.

Almost overnight, I was sprung from my trap. Charlie and I went out every Friday and Saturday night and didn't come back until 2:00 a.m. Suddenly, I had wheels and freedom. We went to all the new movies, ate double-decker hamburgers at Bob's Big Boy, went to the beach, and saw the rock band "Chicago" at the Greek Theatre. And we spent a lot of time parking in the hills next to Starlight Bowl and steaming up the windows of his '65 Mustang.

Dad wasn't totally giving up his control, however. One night, when Charlie and I sat in the Mustang in front of my parents' house until the wee hours, Little Caesar made an unexpected appearance, carrying a flashlight in one hand and a blackjack in the other. Fortunately, I jumped out of the car, and Charlie sped away before any damage was done.

Some months into my new relationship, I started getting good and tired of hearing Little Caesar say, "Where's my napkin?" every night. So, I spent an hour making a papier-mâché napkin holder, then stuffed it full of napkins and set in on the table. There, I said to myself, one less thing he can bug me about. Then, on the day of the napkin holder's debut, when he went into his usual gripe about not having a napkin, I simply pointed to the new device and said, "They're right here." And there it stood—my silly masterpiece, chock-full of napkins and easily within his reach. Little Caesar gave me a murderous look. Clearly, he didn't *want* to get his own napkin—he wanted *me* to fold one and put it under his fork.

169

Furious at my cheekiness, he seized the napkin holder and threw it right in my face. It bounced off the side of my head and fell on the floor beside my chair with a great clatter. As I bent over to pick it up, a red haze clouded my vision. Not giving a damn about the consequences, I picked up the napkin holder and heaved it with all of my might straight at his head. Suddenly, I felt like I'd been pumped full of helium and had risen ten feet off the ground. Woo-hoo! He could have killed me right then, and I would have died with a smile on my face.

To this day, I have no memory of what happened next. But I know I decided, once and for all, I would never let anyone treat me with such blatant disrespect again.

My relationship with Charlie, so euphoric during the spring and summer, began to peter out in the fall. My goals from the start were to be the nicest, sweetest, most wonderful girlfriend in the world. He was my "everything," and I would never give him any reason not to love me. What I didn't understand was my passive, romantic stance didn't ensure he would treat me the same way—it probably did just the opposite.

As time went by, he got more controlling and more insulting. He was forever telling me I was stupid. And, for some inexplicable reason, his nickname for me was "schlemiel," which I found out years later meant an inept, clumsy person. Toward the end of our relationship, he actually slapped my face—even Dad had never done that. But I never challenged him about any of this. I just kept believing that if I was nice enough and pliable enough, he'd always want me.

Eventually, he dumped me for another girl.

Thank God.

∞

In 1974, four years after she first set foot in a classroom, Mom finally bought her own car, a landmark move that increased her independence by leaps and bounds. In the past she'd always had to drop what she was doing in the classroom at 4:00 p.m. and run to the parking lot, where Dad was waiting. But with a car of her own, she could putter around in the classroom after school for as long as she wanted. And on weekends she was free to shop, visit a museum, see a movie, or do anything else she pleased.

By then, I was free, too, away at college in San Diego, with a car, a job, and an apartment of my own. Dad no longer had power over me. When I came home to visit, Mom and I took long walks together, strolling through Descanso Gardens, wandering around the beautiful grounds of Huntington Library, or hiking in the local mountains.

Because we were beyond the parent/child power struggles, we were free to be good friends. And it was during these jaunts that I got to know her better.

I griped to her plenty about Dad, and although she tried to smooth things over by telling me, "I know he loves you very dearly," I didn't really believe her.

She smiled a little sadly then, and added, "Well, he *is* hard to live with, no doubt about it."

171

Then she told me about taking him to a recent faculty dinner, where he'd picked a verbal fight with one of her colleagues.

"I had to drag him away in the middle of the meal," she said, mortified.

"Booze?"

"Of course. I decided then and there I'd never take him to another school function."

I waited for a moment, then asked delicately, "Did you ever think about divorce?"

"Divorce?! Oh, no, divorce is such a terrible thing for the family. Besides, where was I going to go? And what was I going to do? I had no job, no money, and two kids!"

"Well, what about going back to North American? You had your math background."

She responded with a laugh without a trace of humor.

"North American?! I hadn't been there in twenty years! Everything was totally different. No, they wouldn't have wanted me at that point, math background or not."

So, she was stuck. But that was then. Now, Mom was no longer beholden to Dad, and no longer felt the need to stand by silently while he raged.

I saw an unmistakable sign of their changed relationship later that night. Little Caesar got up to his old tricks, storming, swearing, and slamming cupboards. But Mom, up to her eyeballs in math tests that needed grading, was utterly unimpressed. She ignored him for as long as she could, until finally, without even looking up from her papers, she shouted, "Oh, shut up and go to bed!"

And by God, he did.

After he disappeared down the hall, I jumped off the couch and fist-pumped the air!

∞

In 1976, the year of the bicentennial, Mom took her first trip to Europe—without Dad. An educational travel organization was looking for teachers who could recruit students for trips abroad, then accompany them as their counselor. If a teacher signed up eight students, she could take the trip for free. If she got more, they would actually pay her. And even if she only signed up a few kids, she could get a large discount on her own fare.

Well, that lit a fire under my mother, especially since these weren't dinky little trips to cheap places. The kids went to fantastic places like Spain, Austria, Switzerland, Ireland, and other exotic locales, and the trips lasted from three to five weeks!

Mom rounded up five of her best former students (all boys, around sixteen years old), paid a paltry $500, and blasted off on a five-week trip to Spain, where kids and teachers alike studied Spain's language, history, culture, cooking, dancing, and art.

*Arriba, arriba!*

Surprisingly, Dad was okay with this. He had never been much interested in traveling and certainly didn't want to be dragged along on some school trip. But he knew that Mom was dying to travel and see the world, and this was the only way it was going to happen, so he was gracious enough to let her go.

I remember the night she came home from that trip to Spain. Dad and I met her at LAX, and she was absolutely electric with excitement, so wired that she was almost vibrating. I barely recognized her. She had dropped ten pounds from her slim frame during those five weeks because she was so exhilarated. Like a caged animal finally set free, Mom was on an adrenaline high.

Through this same student travel organization, she would eventually visit Austria, Germany, Scotland, England, Italy, and Scandinavia and take a cruise on the western Mediterranean. After a while, she would jettison the student travel groups (too much responsibility and worry), but would continue to travel on her own or in groups. Eventually, she would visit and spend time on every continent in the world.

By the end of the 1970s, Mom's teaching career was flourishing and she was rapidly climbing the pay scale. Teachers' raises were calculated according to years on the job plus continuing education units, and while Mom didn't have a lot of years, she could certainly rack up those units. As a result, she was always taking classes in math, language, education, psychology, or any of a score of other subjects. Yet, she never skated through any class, no matter how silly or boring it might be.

One summer, Mom took a Spanish class and sat in her easy chair every night with her Spanish book on her lap and a tape recorder by her side. Absolutely determined to get an A, she doggedly listened to those language tapes, repeating the words and phrases over and over again.

Finally, unable to hold my tongue, I said, "You know, Mom, you only have to get a C in order to get credit for the class. Why are you killing yourself to get an A?"

She looked up for a moment, then replied blithely, "Oh, I don't know. Personal pride, I guess."

Then it was back to her studying, without missing a beat. That was her, all right.

Over time, Mom would take enough classes to reach the very top of the teaching pay scale. And, by the time she retired, no teacher in LAUSD with the same amount of years on the job as Mom earned a larger paycheck.

∞

That was Mom's life; here's how mine went. Like her, I blossomed, at least somewhat, once I moved away from home and escaped the oppression of living with Dad.

One of the first things I did was go back to ballet class to take lessons from the same teacher Dad had wrenched me away from seven years earlier. I don't think he cared anymore since I was grown up and on my own. But *I* did. And the moment I took my place at the barre, I knew I was home. Ever since, I've taken at least three dance classes a week, and, hopefully, always will.

As for making my way in the world, I pretty much had to start at rock bottom. I had zero self-esteem, no sense of who I was at the core, and no relationship skills other than being nice, sweet, and pliable. If I got angry, I submerged it. If I wanted something, no one knew because, afraid of being rejected, I didn't ask. Resentment bubbled up inside of me, but I had no way to express it. After years of being denigrated by Dad and watching Mom model passivity, I had a lot to learn.

After the big disappointment with Charlie, the driving force in my life became the fear of getting trapped. I'd done all the things I thought a good girlfriend should, and they had landed me right back where I started—scorned, slapped, and rejected. I began to believe that all men were like that. Suddenly, the romantic, dreamy young girl I used to be became suspicious and vigilant.

I mostly dodged the men who were interested in me. When I did go out with someone, if he seemed too interested, I got nervous and bailed. If he drank hard liquor or anything other than an occasional beer, I ran. If he liked recreational drugs, well, forget it. I was definitely not getting involved with anyone who might become an alcoholic or an addict.

Thus began my apprehensive twenty-year journey through the dating world: a long succession of dates that went nowhere, false starts, mini-relationships that lasted a few weeks to a few months, and four or five "real" relationships that went on for about a year apiece. And after each one ended, I added a few more things to my lists of what I wanted from a man and what I absolutely wouldn't accept. The lists just got longer.

My work life followed a similar path. I couldn't seem to

commit to anything: I took acting classes, voice-over workshops, and wrote some screenplays. I worked as a waitress, bank teller, office worker, and substitute teacher, but nothing ever stuck.

Finally, I got a job as an executive assistant at a movie studio, but even then, I "floated" from executive to executive, working as a "permanent temp." The couple of times I actually signed on permanently with someone taught me that once they had me, they took me for granted and abused me. I was having none of that.

And that was the way I lived for years—bouncing from relationship to relationship and from office to office, keeping all of my relationships pleasant but superficial and disappearing the minute things started to heat up. It wasn't fulfilling. It didn't encourage my growth or the development of my talents. And it certainly didn't feed my soul. But it was safe.

During the summer of 1987, Dad developed a particularly nasty cough and felt unusually weak. A trip to the doctor and the resultant lung biopsy revealed that he had inoperable lung cancer.

It wasn't all that surprising. He'd been puffing his way through two-and-a-half packs of unfiltered Camels every day for nearly half a century. We'd all spent years choking on the smoke inside our house and car, and the ashtrays scattered throughout our house were always loaded with cigarette butts. So no one was truly shocked.

He was given six to twelve months to live.

It turned out to be only six, and he spent all of them at home, with hospice care in the end. Mom took a leave of absence from teaching, which was absolutely necessary because, true to form, Dad was a demanding patient. He often rang the bell next to his bed at 2:00 a.m. and ordered her to light him a cigarette, even though his oxygen tank was sitting just two feet away. Naturally, she'd light one for him and sit there for the twenty or thirty minutes it took for him to smoke it before she could go back to bed.

She never thought of saying no.

All three of us were with Dad on the last morning of his life when he died in his own bed. Within half an hour, the mortician came, Mom signed some papers, and they took Dad's body away. The minute he was gone, Mom jumped up, gathered every ashtray she saw, and threw them in the trash can outside.

"No one is ever going to smoke in my house again," she announced, utterly determined.

She got no argument from us.

After that, Dawn and I helped her haul two suitcases full of Dad's clothes, which she had packed weeks earlier, out to the garage to await pickup by the Salvation Army.

Then the three of us went out to lunch.

CHAPTER TEN

# I'll Walk Alone

It wasn't long after Dad's death—a week, maybe two—that Lyndon's pictures and war medals made an unexpected and stunning appearance on our hallway wall.

Headed down the hall in search of a book, I was stopped short by a framed photo of a guy who looked like David Niven hanging next to a collection of our family pictures. He was wearing a soldier's uniform and sitting in front of a painted, East Indian-style backdrop. A second picture showed the same guy in front of the same backdrop, sitting next to two other soldiers.

Directly beneath these pictures, in a neat horizontal row, were four war medals, tacked up individually, one of which was the Purple Heart.

Mom happened to be coming down the hallway when I made this discovery, and I looked at her in astonishment.

"Is that *him*?"

"Yep."

All I could say was, "Wow. You put him on the wall."

She smiled. "Well, he *was* my husband. And I think he deserves some recognition, don't you?"

I had to admit she had a point. How weird, though. We hadn't had a conversation about Lyndon in almost two decades.

**One of the pictures of Lyndon
that hung in our hallway after Dad's death**

And I'd never seen any pictures of him, other than the one taken on their wedding day. Then, suddenly, there he was. I guess there was no point in keeping him a secret any longer.

During the following year, there were more surprises. Mom brought out the old wedding and engagement rings that Lyndon had given her, and alternated between wearing his rings and Dad's. And she began chatting about him spontaneously, talking about canoeing on Como Park Lake, their rushed-up wedding during Lyndon's two-week leave, and their weeks of newly-wedded bliss in North Carolina.

After nearly forty-five years of keeping his existence undercover, Mom suddenly acknowledged Lyndon's rightful place in her life. And, although she wasn't what you'd call the emotionally expressive type, during that spring and summer, she grieved for both of her husbands in her own way. After that, she was ready to move on.

Lyndon's pictures, however, stayed on the wall.

In June 1989 Mom's teaching career concluded the same way it had begun, with a teacher's strike. She could have retired right after Dad's death the previous year, but the strike was brewing, and she thought it might be worth hanging in there for another year. She was right. The nine-day strike rewarded the teachers with a 24 percent pay hike, to be spread out over the next three years. Mom retired just one month after this stunning victory with a considerable bump-up in pay.

And that wasn't the only savvy financial decision she made. As soon as she started teaching, she began investing part of her paycheck in the stock market, and over time, her portfolio grew. Then, when the stock market boomed in the 1990s, she rode the wave and doubled, tripled, even quadrupled her investment.

The upshot was that after retirement, Mom was in far better financial shape than she had ever been in her life. With a paid-off house and car, a decent pension payment, lifetime medical insurance, and a rapidly growing investment portfolio, she had more money than she would ever be able to spend. After years of scrimping, saving, and worrying, money was no longer an issue.

Of course, that didn't mean she changed her frugal Depression Era ways.

She continued to re-use old wrapping paper and ribbon, squirrel away pieces of string, hang her laundry on a clothesline because she refused to buy a dryer, and drive miles out of her way to save twenty-five cents on a pound of chicken.

Once, when we were shopping at Trader Joe's, Mom stood for an inordinately long amount of time in front of a fruit bin. When I came over to see what was going on, she mused, "Hmmm. Which should I get? Peaches or plums?"

She was weighing the pros and cons very seriously.

"Mom!" I exclaimed, exasperated. "I think you can afford both!"

"No, no. Not both," she insisted. "I can only get *one*. I have to choose."

Old habits die hard.

She went with the peaches.

**Mom and me, 1995**

I got better at romantic relationships as the years went by. My boyfriends got steadily nicer and more respectful. I went back to school, got a master's degree in nutrition, and became a dietitian. I took several trips to Europe, made friends, and developed a better sense of myself. I grew more assertive and spoke my mind more often. But I still didn't meet my future husband until I was nearly forty.

We met at a Toastmasters meeting. I'd been hired to give a series of nutrition seminars and felt like I needed to brush up my public speaking skills. As it happened Barry was the Toastmaster that night: he delivered the opening remarks, introduced the speakers, and kept the meeting moving along. This meant he was up and down all evening performing his Toastmaster duties, and I had plenty of opportunities to see him in action. What struck me most was his sense of humor and the light behind his eyes—I sensed a wittiness and a great gentleness.

It suddenly occurred to me that I could like that guy, and he would never hurt me.

Although the two of us barely spoke, I joined the club that very night and signed up for a river-rafting trip they were taking a few weeks later. Barry and I ended up sitting next to each other in a raft for four straight days. We started talking and chattered away all day and well into the evening all four days. I thought he was kind, smart, empathetic, and funny.

On our first date, Barry taught me the foxtrot in my living room, then took me to a tiny French restaurant at the top of the Beverly Wilshire Hotel for dinner and dancing—what a classy way to start a relationship. At some point, he told me he'd long been looking for someone he could dance with. What he didn't know was I'd been dancing all my life and looking for the same thing.

We took ballroom dancing lessons, made speeches at Toastmasters, went to plays and museums, and had romantic weekends away. Things went from good to great to fantastic. Then Mom told me Barry reminded her of Lyndon—the icing on the cake.

We were married in 1993 and had an all-ballroom-dance reception. To this day, we've never stopped dancing.

Not long after our wedding, I started working on a combined family tree for Barry and myself and discovered the wonders of doing genealogical searches on the Internet. I already had a boatload of material about our family, but looking up names on genealogy sites could produce interesting new information, which was lots of fun.

One day when Mom was visiting me, I typed in "Lyndon Raff" on one of those sites. And lo and behold, a list of people from a certain Raff family of Minnesota popped up.

"Hey, Mom," I said excitedly. "Look at this—I think it's Lyndon's family! Were his parents named Frank and Josephine?"

She came closer and peered at the computer screen.

"Yes," she replied vaguely, without much enthusiasm. "That's his family."

"No kidding! Did you keep in touch with them at all?"

"No. I had no contact with them after the war."

Then she went back to her newspaper.

I read the names of his brothers and sisters aloud.

"Leroy, Alton, Evelyn, Arlean spelled in a strange way, and Willis. Now there's a weird name. Willis Raff."

She didn't reply.

I guess we all expected her to last forever, if we ever allowed ourselves to think about it. But in 1996, right around the time she turned seventy-five, Mom started having trouble finding the right word.

She'd be telling a story or asking a question, when suddenly she'd get stuck, and say in an exasperated tone, "Hmmpf, what's the name of that thing?" or "Oh, *you* know what I mean!" The names of everyday objects, people she used to know, actors, politicians and places she'd once visited often escaped her.

Dawn and I became very skilled at guessing and supplying the missing words. And, because Mom's vocabulary was pretty extensive, she could often describe objects even when she couldn't name them. She might say, for example, "Larry came by to fix my...um...my *system of irrigation* in the backyard..."

"Sprinklers!" one of us would shout.

"Yes, sprinklers!" she would laugh, happy to grab the elusive word. It might have been amusing if it weren't so disconcerting.

And then other disturbing things began to happen. Mom left her purse at the grocery store. She got into a few fender benders. She lost her keys. She burned a pot on the stove. She seemed more and more confused.

Clearly, it was time for a visit to the neurologist.

After a series of simple tests—questions like, What city is this? Who is the President? Can you count backwards from 100? How many animals can you name?—the "probable" diagnosis was

Alzheimer's disease. A true diagnosis could only be made upon autopsy. The doctor handed Mom a prescription for Aricept and told her to come back in two months. Aricept was supposed to slow the downslide—and maybe even give her a "bump up" for a couple of months. But it wasn't a cure.

Surprisingly, the combination of the medication and Mom's determination to fight the disease worked well for the first six months. She did get a "bump up" and almost seemed to be her old self again.

I knew, however, that we needed to get her out from behind the wheel before she caused an accident. So, when her driver's license came up for renewal, and the DMV called her in to take a driving test, I was elated. They could be the ones to tell her she couldn't drive anymore, once she flunked that test.

Ever the diligent student, Mom threw herself into studying traffic rules and regulations, just like she did when she was taking classes to move up the teacher's pay scale. I knew she didn't have the slightest chance of passing the test, but didn't discourage her and drove her to the DMV on the appointed day. Then I waited for forty-five minutes while she sweated over a test that most people finish in ten.

To my immense surprise, Mom passed the test—missing only *one* answer!

Stunned at the results and so proud of her, I figured she'd earned the right to keep driving for a little bit longer. That day, she slid happily behind the wheel and drove home in triumph.

But over time, the relentless disease process continued. One day, as I was going through her bills and writing out checks, she sat on the edge of her bed watching me. After a few moments, she said sadly, "You know, I looked at my old math books yesterday. And it's *all* gone..."

She passed a hand in front of her face as if wiping a slate clean. "I don't understand any of it."

I looked at her mournful face. Her trusty math ability, the skill that had always made her special, different, and eminently employable, had finally deserted her. A pain stabbed my heart.

"Oh, Mom," I said sympathetically. "*Nobody* understands that stuff. Now you can finally join the rest of us."

But that, of course, wasn't the point.

∞

Eventually, she had to give up driving and move somewhere more practical. We found a retirement community near Dawn and put our family home up for sale.

But before we could sell the house, Mom and I had to face the herculean task of sorting through a lifetime's worth of possessions—things that were stashed in our closets, cupboards, file cabinets, and a dusty, jam-packed garage.

We spent many days packing up dishes, books, clothes, and the like before we finally turned our attention to the worst task, cleaning out the garage. Mostly, we just threw the stuff away—old dog leashes, rusted tools, jars full of nails, cans of dried-up paint, and boxes of papers, all laden with at least an inch of gritty dust. Whatever was left went to charities or recycling.

At long last, we seemed to have cleared out just about everything, except for some miscellaneous stuff up in the rafters. I climbed a ladder and poked my head above the cross beams to investigate. There were several dusty old boxes up there, plus a few ratty shutters and a large, fluffy roll of pink insulation. But way over to the side, behind the insulation, I could see the edge of a large, old-fashioned, olive green trunk.

"Hey, there's a trunk up here!" I yelled down to Mom. "What's in it?"

"I don't know," she replied blankly, seemingly unaware of its existence.

"Should I grab it? Do you want to see what's inside?"

"Sure," she said amiably.

Of course, "grabbing" the trunk was easier said than done. But after repositioning the ladder a few times, wrenching my back, and tipping over a few boxes that crashed to the ground, I finally managed to pull the trunk out of the rafters and, with Mom's help, set it safely on the garage floor.

It was an old military footlocker, with three big black latches and "U.S. Army" stenciled in black paint on its top and sides. It's probably Dad's old war stuff, I thought.

Mom didn't seem surprised to see it, but she also didn't seem to know what was inside.

We hauled the trunk into the house, pried open the latches, and raised the creaky lid. After pulling away some ancient-looking tissue paper, I saw a neatly folded piece of sunset-colored fabric with a Chinese design. When I carefully lifted it up for inspection, I saw it was a Chinese-style robe made of brocade with red, orange, fuchsia, and gold threads woven through it in an elaborate floral design.

"Whoa! Where did this come from?" I asked, amazed.

The brocade was so stiff and scratchy that I couldn't imagine wearing the robe for more than two minutes. But it was magnificent.

"Lyndon," Mom replied simply.

"Oh my God! Is this the one he sent you from China?"

I remembered her telling me about this years earlier, when I was a teenager.

She smiled and nodded.

"Did you ever wear it? It's fantastic!"

A vague look came over her face as she tried to remember. "I don't think so."

"I think you said it was too scratchy. Do you remember?"

"Yes," she said as she ran her hand slowly over the fabric. Then she added, "But I looked at it a lot."

After folding the robe carefully and putting it aside, I went back to the trunk and kept digging.

The next discovery, wrapped in tissue paper, was a faded white velvet evening bag covered with tarnished and worn silver and gold embroidery. The bag was falling apart, but it had obviously been exquisite at one point.

When I looked at her inquiringly, she picked up the bag and frowned.

"I think it came from somewhere near that big white palace..." Her voice trailed off.

"In India? You mean the Taj Mahal?"

"Yes." She paused for a moment. "That's all I know."

Their wedding album was also there, a thin, spiral-bound notebook that included a picture of a happy young couple leaving the church, with the groom grinning like a Cheshire cat.

Stashed inside were some loose pictures of Lyndon in uniform and a few of him and Mom together, plus a yellowed newspaper clipping of his obituary.

And pressed between two pages at the back of the wedding album was a Western Union telegram dated June 12, 1943.

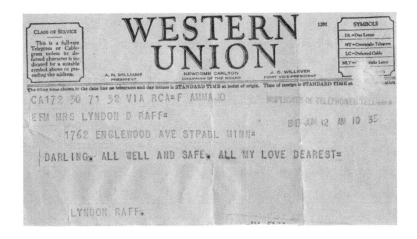

Faded with age but still legible, it was addressed to Mrs. Lyndon Raff and read: *Darling. All well and safe. All my love dearest. - Lyndon Raff*

The last thing I lifted out of the trunk was a small blue leather box that was snapped securely shut.

As I pushed the lid up with my thumbs, a ray of sunlight coming through our kitchen window bounced off the object inside the box and flashed into my eyes. I had to blink and look again.

And there it lay: a silver pin shaped like a pair of wings, with a tiny shield at its center.

I handed the pin to Mom, and a glint of recognition came into her eyes.

"Ahhh, yes, the wings," she said tenderly as she cradled them in her hand. "I wore them all the time."

Then she looked at me with a sad little smile.

"They were supposed to bring him home to me."

We always said that Mom got a "get out of jail free" card when she departed this earth. Hers came in the form of uterine cancer, which made its first appearance in the spring of 2000. If you had to get cancer, they told us, this was the "best" kind because the uterus keeps the cancer cells contained. A simple hysterectomy will take away both the organ and the cancer, leaving nothing behind that can spread.

The surgery was considered very routine, and the doctor predicted that Mom would be home in a couple of days and back on her feet in a week.

But at some point during the operation, her blood pressure skyrocketed and burst a blood vessel in her brain, triggering a sizeable stroke that paralyzed her left side. And she didn't come out of the anesthetic. She was still alive, but in a coma.

After a few days, we decided that keeping her alive with a broken mind and broken body was not only senseless but cruel.

She was transported to a nursing home, where we instructed the doctor to remove hydration and all other kinds of support. It was a Wednesday night, and he told us she probably wouldn't live through the weekend.

We just had to wait for her heart to stop beating.

Two nights later, I got a phone call from Dawn at the nursing home.

"Mom woke up!" she shouted, stunned. "She looked at us and felt our faces!"

What were we supposed to do now?

To me, there was only one answer: "We stay the course." She was still broken in mind and body. And she had told us repeatedly she did not want to be kept alive under circumstances like these. After some discussion, we finally agreed to do nothing.

The weekend came and went while Mom drifted in and out of consciousness. On Monday we put her on a morphine drip to make sure she wasn't in pain. Then on Tuesday, as I sat beside her waiting for the end, she suddenly woke up. And in spite of the stroke, she managed to speak.

"Wha' happened?" she asked, looking at me through glazed eyes.

"Well," I said as gently as I could, "during the operation, you had a stroke."

Then, hoping she wouldn't be afraid or upset, I added, "But it's going to be okay; don't worry about a thing. Pretty soon, it will all be over. No more Alzheimer's. No more stroke. No pain. No problems."

Because she seemed to accept the fact that she was dying, I continued.

"Just think, Mom, you'll see Dad again. And Grandma and Grandpa."

I went on to name a few more people, anybody I could think of who she'd loved who had also passed on. But she didn't respond to any of these names.

Then, almost as an afterthought, I added, "And you'll see Lyndon."

At this, a slow, joyous smile began to spread across her face, and her eyes took on a shine.

"Sounds wonderful," she replied softly.

By the next morning, she was gone.

## CHAPTER ELEVEN

# Finding the Raff Family

A week after Mom's memorial, I sat on the floor of her apartment, sorting through her things and wrapping up her life. Although we'd done the bulk of the work ten months earlier in preparation for her move, there were still plenty of odds and ends to take care of and decisions to make.

Dawn and I picked out a few pictures and decorative items to keep for ourselves, and most of the furniture was set aside for the grandkids, who would be moving into their own apartments soon. The rest was earmarked for the workers at the retirement home, the Salvation Army, or the trash bin. But first, it all had to be organized.

I made piles of things to keep, things to give away, and things to throw out, and had no trouble assigning most of her belongings to one of them. But I stopped in my tracks when I came across Lyndon's medals, photographs from India, and other war memorabilia, which had been bundled together with the wedding album and tied up with ribbon. What was I supposed to do with them?

I told myself sternly that it was time to be realistic and put romanticism aside. Obviously, Lyndon had been very important to Mom, but he didn't really belong to *us*. Stashing his war medals and wedding album in Dawn's attic and pasting his pictures into our family album didn't really make sense.

But I certainly couldn't throw them out.

In an ideal world, I'd locate Lyndon's family and send all of his possessions back to them. But after almost fifty-seven years, who knew where they were—or even if any of them were still alive? Mom told me the last time she'd heard from anyone in the Raff family was a few months after Lyndon's death, when his brother Bill paid her a quick visit while on leave.

With no answers to any of these questions, I simply packed up Lyndon's things and brought them home with me. Later, I thought, when I had more time, I'd figure out what to do with them.

Earlier in the year, we had planned to take Mom back to Minnesota in October to see the farms where her parents had been born, visit South St. Paul and St. Paul proper, and see relatives and old friends. At the time she had enough brain power to connect with people and places, especially those from the past, but it was fast disappearing.

Then, when she suddenly slipped away in August, my first instinct was to cancel the trip. But the more Barry and I talked about it, the more we liked the idea of taking the trip in Mom's place almost as if we were her ambassadors.

It would be fun. We could visit her favorite haunts and imagine what they must have been like when she was there. We could see the people she loved and tell them how much they had meant to her. And we could spread her ashes in her home state.

With more reasons to go than stay home, Barry and I took off for Minnesota with Mom's ashes sealed in a plastic Ziploc bag and tucked away in my carry-on luggage.

The trip turned out to be a joyous, healing time. Dawn came for part of it, during which the three of us visited relatives and some of Mom's old friends and reminisced about the old days. We saw the tiny clapboard house Mom had lived in as a child in South St. Paul. We stopped in at Hamline Methodist Church, where she had regularly attended Sunday services and married Lyndon. And we visited the two farms that still belonged to members of the family.

And then it was time to lay Mom to rest. At the family cemetery, just down the road from the Ostrom farm, I opened the plastic bag and began to sprinkle ashes over every grave that bore a name I recognized, including our great-great-grandparents. Walking up and down the rows between the headstones, pouring slowly, I made sure that Mom's ashes lasted until I had baptized every last grave, a total of at least thirty.

Then we stood in silence and watched the autumn wind pick up her ashes, swirl them around, and sweep them gently across a nearby field. Mom had returned to the very place where she had begun.

∞

At the end of our four-day visit to Minnesota, Barry and I had about an hour to kill before leaving for the airport and decided to spend it at the nearby Minnesota Historical Society. It was a fun and interesting place full of colorful exhibits, including one that looked at South St. Paul's meatpacking industry.

Since Grandpa had spent forty years working in the packing plants, I really should have been fascinated by this display. But for some reason, Barry and I passed through it fairly quickly and ended up wandering downstairs. There, quite unexpectedly, we found ourselves in the Reading Room.

Obviously, we didn't have time to do any reading, so I just drifted aimlessly past shelf after shelf of books, idly reading the titles printed on their spines. And then my gaze fell upon a book titled *Pioneers in the Wilderness*.

Hmmm, I thought. That sounds like my ancestors.

I pulled the book off the shelf and turned it around so I could read the cover. The author's name, spelled out in yellow block letters, was Willis H. Raff.

It took a second or two before my brain registered the name.

Then, stunned by my discovery, I almost shouted, "Oh my God, Barry! Look at this! It's Lyndon's brother!"

It *had* to be him. Who else had that very strange name? And, according to the book jacket copy, he had been born in 1921 and received a degree from Hamline University.

I couldn't tell from his bio whether or not he was still alive, but if he was, maybe his publisher would tell me how to contact him. I scribbled down the title of the book and the publisher's name straight away.

As soon as we got home, I eagerly dashed off a note to the publisher asking for Willis Raff's contact information. But weeks and then months went by with no reply. And I had absolutely no idea how to continue my search.

Strange as it may sound today, in the year 2000, people didn't Google each other at the drop of a hat and get results; that idea was still in its infancy. So, I was simply flummoxed for an entire year.

Then one day, it occurred to me that if I typed "Willis Raff" into a search engine, I just might find something. When I did, I found that not only was he still alive, he was lecturing in Grand Marais, a small city in northeastern Minnesota!

I instantly emailed the Grand Marais post office and was rewarded the very next day with his address. I sat down and wrote to him immediately.

> *Dear Mr. Raff,*
>
> *You don't know me, but my mother was Nina Ostrom, your brother Lyndon's wife. My mother passed away last year and I have some things that were Lyndon's that I thought you might want, including his WWII medals. I also have their wedding album, some other pictures of Lyndon or the two of them, a telegram that he sent her, his obituary, etc.*

*I'd be happy to send you the medals and copies of whatever you'd like to have … Just say the word and I'll send you lots of things.*

*Happy Veteran's Day!*

His reply came a few weeks later:

*Dear Mrs. Fox:*

*What a wonderful surprise to get your good letter yesterday! So many years have gone by since Lyndon's marriage and death that I had no real reason to hope. You open a whole new level of knowledge and expectation!*

*The last time I saw your mother was a few weeks after we learned that her husband had been killed flying cargo planes from India over Burma, to help the Chinese in their struggle with the Japanese. As I was then in the Air Corps at McClellan Air Force Base near Sacramento, with a 3-day pass I was able to visit and spend some time with her in Los Angeles… …Since that time I never had any contact with your mom or knowledge of her later life, although somehow I did learn that she had remarried.*

*Yes! I would be profoundly grateful if you could send my brother's papers, medals, photos, obituary, etc., etc. ...*

*Two of Lyndon's older brothers have died; his two sisters are still alive, one in San Francisco, the other in Munich, Germany. Believe me, dear lady, they will join me in being eternally grateful for whatever you send!!*

*Sincerely,*
*Bill*

I carefully pinned Lyndon's four war medals to a white satin rectangle: the Air Medal (for distinguished meritorious achievement in flight); the Distinguished Flying Cross (for more than fifty operational flights through combat zones); the Oak Leaf Cluster (for more than seventy-five missions with probable and expected exposure to enemy fire); and the Purple Heart (for being wounded or killed in action). I put the medals inside a necklace case and slid it into a FedEx box.

Next, I added a manila envelope containing Lyndon's pictures, obituary, and telegram to Mom, plus a copy of the eulogy from Mom's funeral, just in case the Raffs wanted to know what happened to the girl who was once part of their family. Last, I eased in the slim wartime wedding album and sealed the FedEx box with too much packing tape. Precious cargo, I thought—all that's left of Lyndon.

I sent the package to Bill Raff's home in early December 2001. He reported that after going through its contents very carefully, he sent the package to his sister Evelyn, who sent it on to their other sister, Arlean.

By Christmas Day, Lyndon had paid a visit to every one of his surviving siblings.

The last Christmas he'd spent with his family was in 1941, on the heels of the bombing of Pearl Harbor, just a few weeks before he joined the Army Air Forces. Sixty years later, Lyndon came home for the holidays one more time.

Once I got word that Lyndon's package had arrived, I never expected to hear from the Raff family again. But six years later, in January 2008, out of the blue, I got a letter from Lyndon's niece, Dixie, daughter of his brother, Alton.

She told me Bill Raff had died about nine months after I'd sent him Lyndon's war memorabilia, and Dixie had "inherited" it. She thought it would be fun to get together and chat about our families. And since she was in southern California on a visit, lunch was a possibility.

I jumped at the chance, and we set a date.

Charming and easy to talk to, Dixie confided that she was only five years old when her Uncle Lyndon died and had no memories of him, but she had always idolized him because of what she'd heard from family members.

"They all said he was the star of the family," she recalled. "The smartest, the best-looking, and the nicest of the bunch."

That certainly jibed with what Mom had told me.

"I totally romanticized him," she continued. "As a child, I used to look at an observatory glinting in the sun on top of some nearby mountains and imagine that was where his plane had crashed." She thought about him all the time and even named her first-born son Lyndon.

The conversation flowed pretty easily, and somehow we got on the topic of Lyndon's life insurance money. I knew all about how Mrs. Raff didn't give Mom a penny, but I'd decided in advance not talk about that. I was surprised Dixie knew anything about it.

"Oh yes," she recalled, "that life insurance money was very important to my grandmother. She really wanted to be the biggest donor at Hamline Church, which was a great honor. And that's what she did with the money; she donated every last penny to the church."

Not wanting to stir up a hornet's nest, I decided to change the subject to something I'd been wondering about for a while. While cleaning out Mom's things, I'd found a letter from the Army informing her that Lyndon's burial would take place in January 1950. That seemed like an awfully long time after his death in 1943.

"Okay, here's a question for you, Dixie," I began. "Lyndon was killed in October 1943, but he wasn't brought back to the

States until 1950. Why do you think it took so long?"

My question was rhetorical, not really a request for information. How should she know why it took over six years to bring her uncle home again?

But Dixie's reply, so focused and assured, made my jaw hit the floor.

"Well," she said lightly, "Since all nine soldiers were buried in a mass grave, the Army needed permission from nine families to exhume them and bring them home for burial. And they *did* get permission from everyone, except ..."

She paused for a moment. "...except *your* mother."

I looked at her blankly.

"She refused," Dixie explained. "And that's why the bodies of all nine guys had to stay in India. They weren't brought back until my grandparents proved that your mom had remarried, and they were able to reclaim next of kin rights. *That's* why it took six years."

She might just as well have told me that I had two heads. Her outrageous statement simply didn't compute.

"No, no, no," I insisted, totally rejecting the idea. "She *loved* Lyndon. She didn't want him rotting in some graveyard in India!"

Dixie just shrugged. "Well, that's what *I* heard."

"Besides," I continued, "she was nothing like that! My mom was a 'get-alonger' who always went with the flow. She would *never* have dug her heels in about something like that!"

204

Images of Mom, the model of passivity, flashed through my mind. There she was, standing by and doing nothing while Dad bullied Grandpa, ripped Dawn's blouse, and threw a napkin holder in my face. *This* was the woman who refused to let the Army bring home nine dead soldiers? Unthinkable.

"And she would never have stood in the way of other people bringing their sons home!" I almost shouted.

Dixie simply raised an eyebrow and said nothing.

It was absolutely, utterly impossible.

I knew my mother better than anybody, and there was no way in hell she would have said, "Forget it. I don't want you bringing my husband home from India. And if that means his fellow soldiers have to stay there too, well, so be it."

Dixie's assertion was the most preposterous thing I had ever heard in my life. But I had to wonder: were there more secrets to this story yet to be discovered?

∞

As soon as I got home from that lunch, I called Dawn to tell her what Dixie had said about Mom.

"Gee," she said thoughtfully, "do you think Mom might have been mad enough about that insurance money to refuse to bring Lyndon home?"

"What?! Not a chance! I don't think she gave a hoot about that money."

"Well," Dawn replied, "I know that *Grandma* was really ticked off about it."

Grandma? I'd never heard anything about *her* take on the insurance issue.

"Yes, don't you know that? Grandma was really steamed that Mom lost out on that money. She always thought Lyndon's mother should at least have given her *something*."

Suddenly, a crazy thought struck me. Could *Grandma* have been angry enough to stand in the way of bringing those soldiers home?

When Barry got home that afternoon, I told him what went on at lunch, ending with my newly formulated idea about what might have happened.

"Think about it: Everything was done by mail in those days. And since Mom was moving around a lot, all of her mail was sent to Grandma's house. Maybe *Grandma* wrote a letter or signed a form in Mom's name, refusing to bring Lyndon home."

Barry, who is not given to flights of fancy, was a bit skeptical.

"But why would your grandmother do that? Why would she hurt Lyndon? Didn't she like him?"

"Yes, she liked him. But can't you see? It would have been the perfect way to get back at Mrs. Raff for screwing Mom out of that money!" "Wow, do you really think she could have done that?"

I *did* think so. Or sometimes I did.

But for the next several days, I was haunted by Barry's question. *Would* Grandma actually do such a thing?

**Josephine Raff (left) and Blanch Ostrom**
**at Nina and Lyndon's wedding - October 1942**

I brought up the subject again at dinner a few nights later, determined to convince Barry I was really on to something.

"Okay, you've got to agree that it couldn't have been Mom who kept those guys from coming home."

"No," he said amiably, "I don't think Nina would have done that. So, yes, I agree."

"And I happen to know that Mom *didn't* have an axe to

grind about the insurance money."

"Really? How do you know?"

"Because she only mentioned it to me twice in all the zillions of conversations we had. If it bugged her, I'm sure I would have heard more about it."

He digested this for a minute.

"Okay, so we both agree it wasn't her. But what makes you think your grandmother did it?"

"Well, she had both opportunity and motive."

Barry and I watched a lot of murder mysteries, and I knew this would be a good way to present my case.

He smiled at me, eyes twinkling.

"Okay, Sherlock, how did it happen?"

"It went like this: Because all of the Army's correspondence to Mom was sent to Grandma's address, Grandma had access to the letters before Mom did. This gave her the opportunity to respond in Mom's name with no one knowing the difference."

"Okay, and how about the motive?"

"Well, Grandma, who could be a real brooder, was furious at Mrs. Raff about the insurance payout. And sitting in the next pew at church every Sunday is Mrs. Raff, getting all kinds of praise for being a big, generous donor. Grandma *had* to get back at her or go crazy!"

"And you think the way she did this was by refusing to bring Lyndon's body home."

"Can't you just see it? One day, Grandma gets a letter from the Army addressed to Mom..."

"And it's the one asking your mom for permission to bring Lyndon's body back to the States," Barry said, finishing my thought.

"Yes! So, Grandma checks off a box on a form that says, 'I deny permission,' then signs Mom's name and sends it back."

"And no one ever found out."

"Right! As long as she never breathed a word about it, it would be her little secret—until now."

There was just one thing that didn't make sense. My parents got married in 1946, and Lyndon's remains weren't returned to the States until 1950. Dixie said the Raffs reclaimed next of kin rights once Mom remarried. So why did it take *four more years* to bring Lyndon's remains home?

"Red tape?" Barry asked.

I rejected that idea. Even red tape didn't take that long.

After much thought, I came up with what seemed like a plausible answer. Since Mom was living in California, Grandma could easily have hidden the news of her remarriage from the folks in Minnesota for a long time. Maybe even until the end of '48, when Mom got pregnant with Dawn. That's when Grandma could have joyfully announced that not only had her daughter remarried, but Grandma was going to be a Grandma!

"So, you're saying the Raffs didn't ask for next of kin rights until your parents had been married for almost three years?"

"Yes, because the Raffs didn't know about the marriage! This means the process of bringing the guys home wouldn't have even *begun* until late '48, ending with their burial in early 1950."

"Well, the timing seems to fit."

And it was a much more logical explanation for the long delay in bringing the soldiers home than Mom digging in her heels for absolutely no reason.

Determined to clear Mom's name, I sat down and wrote a letter to Dixie explaining my perfect theory.

Seven long years would pass before Dixie and I communicated again. In 2015, I decided that I wanted to write a book about Mom and Lyndon, and I needed copies of the memorabilia I'd sent to Bill Raff some fourteen years earlier. Dixie, who by then was living in southern California, generously invited me to her house to look at everything she had.

On that January morning, Barry and I sat expectantly in Dixie's living room, watching her open a big plastic storage box containing the pictures, wedding album, and other items that had once belonged to Mom. And to our great surprise, it also contained twenty-two wartime letters that Lyndon had written to his parents, plus six others he'd written to Bill. Dixie hadn't mentioned anything about any letters during our lunch seven years earlier!

There was also a copy of Lyndon's Army personnel file, with all correspondence regarding Lyndon either to or from the

Army from the time of his death through 1964—twenty-one years.

In addition, Dixie had a "Missing Air Crew Report" and an eyewitness account of the fatal crash.

Both Barry and I were mesmerized by the find. We asked where we could find the nearest copy machine, but, amazingly, Dixie replied, "Oh, just take it all with you and keep it as long as you want."

We instantly jumped up and hauled our unexpected treasure to the car, afraid she might change her mind. And on the drive home, we marveled at our fabulous luck.

"Just think, Barry," I said. "I've got all these letters written in Lyndon's own handwriting that are going to tell me what kind of guy he was and what he was doing, thinking, and feeling during the war!"

He smiled and shook his head. "And Dixie never said a thing, did she?"

"Not a word. Or I would have begged her for copies of this stuff seven years ago."

We rode for a while in silence.

Then I said, "You know what the best part is? I'm going to be able to find out who wrote that damned letter that kept those guys from coming home from India."

"Yeah," Barry agreed. "And why."

We couldn't wait to get home and plunge into that file.

## CHAPTER TWELVE

# Tell Me About My Boy

Until I read the Department of the Army's Individual Deceased Personnel file for Lyndon O. Raff, everything I knew about the dashing pilot who had married my mother was strictly hearsay and, therefore, subject to interpretation.

But documentation that came straight from the government would tell me in no uncertain terms what had happened to him. And he himself would tell me his story through his letters, frayed at the edges, written with a fountain pen, and clamped together with a heavy binder clip.

Barry and I sat at the kitchen table, laid out the contents of the box of treasures Dixie had lent me, then dove into Lyndon's Army file. A quick pass revealed dozens of official documents that ran the gamut from the tediously mundane to the utterly heartbreaking, often in juxtaposition.

For example, mixed in with pages of dental records, all vitally important to the identification of a soldier's remains, was a photocopy of a luggage tag bearing Lyndon's handwriting.

A painstakingly compiled list of his personal effects included items so ordinary they hardly seemed worth mentioning—"1 fountain pen, Schaeffer," "1½ pr. pajamas," "6 pr. socks"—combined with highly precious and personal things like "11 service ribbons," "1 diary," and "4 framed pictures."

"Wow, look at this," I muttered, half to myself. "Here's

his Aviation Cadet physical exam, noting the dates of his childhood measles, mumps, and scarlet fever. And the very next document shows the cause of his death was 'crushing.'"

Barry winced.

But then came the real gold: thirty letters and two telegrams regarding Lyndon either sent or received by the Army. I knew that somewhere in that stack we were going to find the letter, supposedly signed by my mother, that refused to allow Lyndon's remains to be exhumed and returned to the States. And I would instantly know whether it had been signed in Mom's handwriting or Grandma's. Or someone else's.

It was Barry's idea to divide the correspondence into piles according to sender. And to our surprise, we ended up with just two piles: twenty-four letters and two telegrams came from the Army, and six letters came from the Raffs. There wasn't a single letter from Mom.

Then something caught my eye.

"Hey, that's Mom's handwriting!"

At the bottom of a letter written to my mother from the Army on April 21, 1948,, Mom had scribbled an answer before sending it back. The letter said:

*Our office is endeavoring to determine the next*
*of kin of the late First Lieutenant Lyndon O. Raff.*
*Information has been received which indicates*
*that you have remarried. It is requested,*

*therefore, that you inform this office whether you have... in order that our records may be correctly amended.*

Mom had dutifully checked the "yes" box to indicate that she had remarried, then signed her new name and gave her new address.

"And that's when the Army found out your mom had remarried," Barry said, inspecting the letter more closely.

A letter from the Raffs bringing the remarriage to the attention of the Army had to be somewhere in the file. Sure enough, I found one sent a few weeks earlier, on April 8:

*His wife, Nina, married again some two years ago... We do not know if Nina has notified your office that she remarried. Since she is, should any information need to go to her?*

I gleefully handed this second letter to Barry.

"Ha! It looks like it took two years before the Raffs found out about Mom and Dad's marriage. So that means Grandma was *almost* successful in keeping the marriage a secret until Mom got pregnant. Just like I thought!"

Barry scanned the letter, then looked up with a puzzled expression.

"Okay, so they know she's married. But where's the letter from the Army asking for your mom's permission to bring Lyndon's remains home? And where's the letter that refuses?"

Surely letters like these would be so important that copies would have been made in triplicate for the file. They *had* to be there.

We both read all eleven pieces of correspondence sent to Mom by the Army. Not one of them asked for her approval to do anything with her husband's remains or even mentioned the topic.

Then we turned our attention to the six letters sent to the Army by the Raffs, all of which were written by Mrs. Raff.

"If somebody was keeping Mrs. Raff from bringing her son's body home," Barry said, "she has to have mentioned it one of these letters."

"Or screamed it," I agreed.

We carefully read the Raff letters, searching for something along the lines of, "Our daughter-in-law wouldn't allow our son to be brought home for burial. But now that we have next of kin rights, we want to change that."

There was nothing—nothing from the Army asking for permission to bring home Lyndon's remains, nothing from Mom refusing it, and nothing from the Raffs complaining about her supposed refusal.

As for my grandmother, there *was* one document in the file that bore her handwriting. She had signed Mom's name on a shipping bill to acknowledge receipt of Lyndon's personal effects.

However, there was no letter blocking the return of the soldiers' remains signed by Grandma in my mother's name, which effectively ended my theory that *she* might have been the villain. (Sorry, Grandma!)

Once we were completely finished reading the file, Barry and I gloried in the exoneration of my family for a few minutes. Yet I still had to ask:

"But why did it take *six years* to bring Lyndon home?'

Barry shrugged.

"Why don't you Google 'bringing home dead soldiers in World War II?' Maybe you'll find something."

I Googled it. And I found something.

You have to imagine it: World War II had finally come to an end, and the bodies of some 280,000 deceased American soldiers were literally scattered all over the world. While the battles were raging, hardly any of the deceased had been returned to the States. Because the country was funneling everything it had into winning the war, it simply didn't have the time, money, or manpower necessary for shipping bodies home. Instead, fallen soldiers were temporarily laid to rest in U. S. military cemeteries around the world—but only if they happened to die relatively close to one. If they met their deaths in distant or hard-to-access places, they were just buried where they had fallen.

It wasn't until late '45 that the U.S. government set up The Return of the World War II Dead Program. The Army's

Quartermaster General was put in charge and assigned the gargantuan tasks of recovering and identifying the bodies of deceased U.S. soldiers around the world and returning them to their permanent burial sites.

I found a *Wall Street Journal* article titled "How We Bury Our Dead" that explained the entire program.

"Listen to this," I said to Barry. "The Quartermaster General's office not only recovered and identified the bodies, it also informed the families of the whereabouts and status of their loved ones, returned their personal effects, and sorted out the burial details."

"Wow, one office did all those things for 280,000 dead soldiers?"

It did. And the more I read about the program, the more enormous and impossible its tasks seemed to be.

All recoverable remains of U.S. soldiers who died overseas were buried in local military cemeteries, if possible. As for those buried where they had fallen, every attempt was made to recover their remains and bring them back to a military cemetery.

In all cases each body had to undergo an identification procedure before being laid to rest in a military cemetery.

Eventually, the remains were disinterred from the military cemeteries and sent to one of several processing stations around the world, located in the South Pacific, Japan, Hawaii, France, the Netherlands, Italy, and North Africa. There, they went through a second identification process, performed by an anthropologist, using the most advanced scientific techniques available. Only then was identification considered official.

Most of the bodies were fairly easy to identify—they were found with their dog tags, identifying papers, I.D. bracelets, or other jewelry. There may also have been laundry marks on their clothing or other clues.

Still, every physical detail that could be detected was recorded on a chart and, if available, fingerprints and hair samples were taken. Any remaining teeth or portions of the jaw were compared to the soldier's dental charts. If the body was in pieces, the skeleton was reassembled on a table, and a diagram was constructed, indicating bones that were present, as well as those that were missing.

If, after every piece of physical evidence was analyzed and recorded, the anthropologist believed there was enough evidence to establish an individual's identity, a report would be prepared comparing the findings from the lab to the individual's physical records. The report was sent to a board of review, and, if they agreed, it was sent on to a second board of review in Washington, D.C.

If the second board also agreed, positive identification was officially established.

After extensive testing that sometimes utilized every method available, the remains were either considered 100 percent positively identified as a particular individual or "unidentified." There was no such thing as "almost certain" identification.

Remains that were positively identified were then made ready for return to their final resting places, and a letter was sent to the next of kin asking about the desired location. There were four possible choices: a U.S. military cemetery at home, a U.S. military cemetery overseas, a private cemetery at home, or a private cemetery in a foreign country.

Some ninety-four percent of the recovered remains of World War II soldiers were positively identified, and their burials were handled in this manner.

The six percent who were *not* positively identified took a different route. If they were simply unidentifiable, they stayed on a shelf; perhaps a newer technology would be able to identify them one day. If they could be positively identified as two or more people, yet couldn't be separated conclusively as individuals, they were considered "co-mingled."

From that point on, all decisions regarding their disposition would be made solely by the Army. There would be no dividing of remains among the families for burial in their chosen cemeteries. The Army would bury the co-mingled remains as a group in a military cemetery in the U.S. that was about the same distance away from their hometowns.

The wishes of the families would hold no sway.

The story of Lyndon's burial and re-burial is all there in his personnel file; some of it expected, some not. It began, of course, on that sunny day in late October 1943, when the

C-47 he was piloting lost an engine, caught its left wing on some tree tops, and cartwheeled down a hillside in Burma, crashing and exploding in a small wash.

An eyewitness report of the accident described "intense heat from burning gasoline" and noted "eight bodies found in wreckage... none can be identified." Since there were *nine* soldiers on the plane, it seems that the remains of two of them were already co-mingled and appeared as one. The following day at dusk, the soldiers were buried at the scene of the crash, where they would remain for over two years.

Toward the end of 1945, when The Return of the World War II Dead Program was just getting into gear, the Army disinterred Lyndon and his crew from the crash site and brought them down the hill. Their remains were taken to the closest U.S. military cemetery, located in Kalaikunda, India, about twenty-seven miles north of Calcutta.

Once the remains were delivered, the authorities set about identifying them—or what was left of them after two years in a hillside grave without the protection of a casket. It's not clear how bodies were identified at the military cemetery or whether scientific methods were used. But somehow it was decided that one set of the remains belonged to two people: First Lieutenant Lyndon O. Raff and Corporal Max K. Hall, a member of the drop crew. Maybe Lyndon was identified by Mom's high school ring, which he had worn on his right little finger, or by his wedding ring. (He was the only married soldier on board.) Something similar may have identified Max.

Whatever the clues, the authorities were certain the remains belonged to the two of them, but couldn't be separated conclusively, so they were considered a "group." And on December 29, 1945, exactly two years and two months after the crash, they were buried together at the military cemetery at Kalaikunda.

The families of deceased soldiers truly suffered. Not only had they lost their beloved sons, husbands, or brothers, it was often years before they knew where they were or what had happened to them. Lyndon's loved ones offer the perfect example.

A few weeks after the plane crash on October 29, 1943, the MIA and later KIA telegrams were sent, although they said nothing about where or how he died or his place of burial. Mom's telegram simply said her husband had perished in "the Asiatic area." During the next two-and-a-half years, she received nothing more from the Army, other than a shipment of Lyndon's personal effects and his flight record.

The Raffs knew even less. Since all of the Army's correspondence automatically went to the widow, and Mom was completely estranged from the Raffs because of the insurance fiasco, all they knew was their son was KIA in "the Asiatic area."

After about eighteen months of silence, Mrs. Raff was understandably upset. Dying for news and suspecting that Mom was holding back on information, she wrote to the Army and asked to be "put on the mailing list" for information about her son:

*This information may have been sent to his wife, but as we do not hear from her, we are anxious to learn if there has been or will be anything new about where he is buried and if the remains will be returned to his native state after the war...*

In the next paragraph, she got a little bolder, making clear her own preference for Lyndon's place of burial:

*We realize his wife has the last word, but we do not want his remains to be sent anywhere else except to his home city, St. Paul, for burial at Ft. Snelling.*

That very same day, Mrs. Raff wrote to the Army Effects Bureau asking for Lyndon's flight record, adding this comment:

*This record may have been sent to his wife, but as we do not hear from her, we do wish it sent to us too.*

The reply from the Army must have been galling:

*The right of the widow to receive the property supersedes that of the parents; therefore, the flight record... was sent to Mrs. Nina B. Raff.*

Mrs. Raff was successful in persuading the Army to put her on the mailing list, and forever after received the same information that was sent to Mom. In fact, the Raffs were sometimes better informed than she was.

In response to a letter Mrs. Raff had written requesting specific information about her son's remains, the Army reported in September 1945:

*"[They] were interred in the vicinity in which he met his death"* [and] *"are being removed to the nearest established military cemetery."*

It was more than the Army ever told his widow. Mom never knew that Lyndon's plane had crashed in the hills of Burma, or that his remains were buried there for more than two years. She also thought his plane had crashed because it was overloaded and never made it off the runway.

In the spring of 1946, the Army finally got around to informing both Mom and the Raffs that Lyndon had been buried at Kalaikunda. No mention was made of the co-mingled remains; it would be two more years before they learned about this. By then, the group had been disinterred from Kalaikunda and was headed to Hawaii for processing by the Central Identification Laboratory.

"All right, let me see if I've got this straight," I said to Barry. "They spent two years on a hill in Burma, two and a half years in a military cemetery in India, and almost another two years in Hawaii. And whose fault was this?"

"No one's. It was just Army procedure; you know, the old 'hurry-up-and-wait' thing. I guess you could say even the dead had to get in line."

My later research revealed that six years actually wasn't an unusual length of time for the repatriation of deceased World War II soldiers. The very *first* bodies didn't make it back to the U.S. until the fall of 1947, a full two years after the war's end. Lyndon's return, in early 1950, occurred just a little over two years after that. Considering there were some 280,000 bodies to be recovered, identified, buried, and reburied during an era that was pre-computer and low-tech, I guess you really couldn't expect things to go much faster.

∞

By now, it was clear that Dixie's story of Mom's refusal to bring home Lyndon's remains, and those of the eight soldiers who died with him, was completely false. Permission had never been requested in the first place and, in any case, couldn't have been granted or denied by Mom because the remains were government property the minute they were designated "co-mingled." From then on, their fate would be decided solely by the Army.

So, who made up the diabolical story about Mom? Dixie said her father had told her the story, but he wasn't Lyndon's next of kin, so how could he have known the details? He had to have heard the story from his mother. But didn't Mrs. Raff know that the *Army* was in charge of the disposition of her son's remains, not Mom?

I thumbed through the stack of correspondence, looking for a letter from the Army informing the Raffs of the status of their son's remains. I found two, both of which were written in April 1948, when Mom was still officially Lyndon's next of kin.

The first one reported that it wasn't possible to establish individual identification of Lyndon, so he was being buried as part of a group. The second, written just a week later, said the group remains would be returned for final burial to Fort McPherson National Cemetery in Nebraska.

There was no request for permission or the family's preferences.

At the time, the Raffs were knee-deep in the process of taking back next of kin rights due to Mom's remarriage, but it wouldn't matter. The Army was and always would be in charge of the remains.

Still, Mrs. Raff wasn't going down without a fight. She immediately wrote to the Army requesting a change in burial site:

*Would it be possible to have this changed and the final interment be made in Arlington Cemetery at Washington, D.C.? This would seem to be a more central location for the majority of the*

*survivors of the group and more convenient for*
*future visits to the graves of our dead.*

No dice.

The Army had made its decision and wasn't about to change it.

So, there it was. Mrs. Raff had known all along that the Army had decided the fate of Lyndon's remains, not Mom. Yet she lied to her family (and probably her friends), smearing her former daughter-in-law with a story that became so ingrained in family lore that her granddaughter Dixie accepted it as fact.

But why would she tell such a story? It couldn't have been because of the insurance money; she'd won that battle. For some reason, she was furious with Mom and determined to wipe her out of Lyndon's life, even after his death.

A quick scan of some of her letters to the Army shows her vengefulness. In one, she asked:

*Since she is remarried should any information*
*need to go to her?*

In another, she made a biting assumption:

*As a consequence of her remarriage, it can be*
*assumed she is no longer interested in the final*
*disposition of our son's remains...*

Then she added:

*P.S. You might pass on the information of the widow's remarriage to the department making payment of widow's pensions, as she may still be drawing her pension, which we are informed should be terminated at her remarriage.*

This last bit seems particularly malicious, but it didn't make any difference in the end. Mom had never collected any widow's payments in the first place. She'd always made too much money to qualify for them.

Much of the animosity can probably be explained by the grief, frustration, and powerlessness Mrs. Raff felt during those long years of waiting for her boy to come home. Closure was surely impossible when she couldn't lay her son to rest and take comfort in the fact that he was finally back where he belonged. Maybe she just had to strike out at someone.

If so, Mom would have been the obvious candidate because, frankly, Mrs. Raff was jealous of her.

After raising Lyndon, taking care of him, and cherishing him as only a mother could, how did he repay her? He went off and fell in love with a young girl and made her the most important woman in his life! It must have been a bitter pill for Mrs. Raff to swallow, as she obviously resented this young interloper very much.

In the twenty-eight wartime letters written by Lyndon that still survive, there are plenty of clues pointing to her dislike of Mom. It's clear that Lyndon could sense his mother's disapproval, but he seemed determined to forge a connection between her and his girlfriend, later his wife, even in absentia.

In various letters home, he nudged:

*Here's what I'd like you to do... Sometime in the near future have Nina and possibly her folks over for a dinner.*

*... If you should run into Nina on the street sometime, why don't you ask her to stop in some afternoon?*

*She's a little shy and bashful... but now that it's quiet... maybe it'll be a little easier to get better acquainted.*

*Do you ever write to Nina? It might help her a bit if you did drop her a cheery letter once in awhile.*

*Mother, if you go home next summer... would you think it possible you and Nina and maybe Arlean could possibly go on a little trip together?*

In another letter, he confided to his father:

*I'm certainly glad we can start married life away from St Paul... If and when we ever get back to St. Paul <u>together to stay</u> [his emphasis], we will have been together long enough to not need any all-too-well-meant help.*

Of course, it probably didn't help matters much when Mom wrote merrily to her in-laws :

*A man with shaving soap all over his face—I guess it's my husband—just stuck his head in the door and told me to cover up... Guess I'd better get ready for bed.*

Mom was a target for Mrs. Raff's fury, which, of course, was totally unfair. And yet I have to wonder how I would react if I were in Mrs. Raff's shoes.

What if I were the mother of a soldier killed in action while fighting overseas, and three long years passed before I could even find out where he was buried? And how would I feel about waiting six interminable years before he was finally brought home for burial, then being forced to accept a burial place so far from my home that I'd probably never be able to visit him? And how could I face the terrible reality of never seeing his face or hearing his voice again—of losing my beautiful twenty-five-year-old son forever?

I know I'd be furious. And I'd probably be looking for a way to release some of the rage, grief, and disappointment that was consuming my life. Yes, perhaps I'd be in search of a target myself.

∞

I suppose Ft. McPherson National Cemetery was a fair compromise for both families: after all, it was equally inconvenient, if not impossible, for either to visit. Max Hall's hometown of Silt, Colorado, was 450 miles away, a seven-hour trip by car, while the drive from St. Paul took nine hours and covered 646 miles.

It almost didn't matter: the cemetery was so far away it might as well have been on the moon. I know for a fact that Mom never visited Lyndon's grave, and, with one exception, neither did any of his brothers or sisters. Lyndon's parents, however, did manage to make it to his funeral in January 1950, after a very long train ride and an overnight stay.

Unfortunately, according to Dixie, the funeral was an unmitigated disaster.

After all of that agonizing over the proper disposition of the remains and all those years of waiting, the hallowed event turned out to be anything but hallowed. There were just four mourners: both sets of parents. And even though six years had passed since the deaths of the two soldiers, feelings were still raw.

According to Dixie, at some point, one or both of the Halls screamed, "Your son killed our son!" at the Raffs, who recoiled in horror. The entire experience was so upsetting that as soon as the bugler finished playing "Taps," both couples rushed off in broken-hearted agony.

Forty-two years would pass before Lyndon had another visitor.

∞

In November 1992, Bill Raff decided it was high time for him to take a trip to see his favorite brother's grave and pay his respects. He was just twenty-two years old when Lyndon died; now, he was a graying, but still vital, seventy-one-year-old man.

Bill had become more and more interested in the details of his brother's death in recent years and was slowly but doggedly acquiring information about Lyndon from the Army.

He had also been poring over old wartime letters from his brother, written to him and his parents. His mother had saved them and passed them on to Bill when she died. Neither of them could stand the thought of throwing them away.

Bill loved reading them; they made it seem like his brother was still alive. He always had to laugh whenever he thought about that last letter he'd received from Lyndon:

*What are you trying to do? Rub it in with your last line—"I've got to go home to my wife & bed. Damn!!"*

*Just wait till I get back home and you're still overseas someplace. It'll be my turn then.*

*But enough for now, Sargeant.*

So, it was with a smile on his face that Bill set off on that chilly fall morning, bound for Maxwell, Nebraska. The cemetery was 380 miles from his home in South Dakota, and November hardly seemed like a good time for a driving trip. But he went anyway, driving straight through, without stopping, all the way to Fort McPherson National Cemetery. It was time to say both hello and goodbye to Lyndon, at long last.

In a letter about the trip that Bill wrote to his remaining siblings, he described the cemetery and the things he did there:

*It took only a short walk to locate his marker. Very nice and traditional, the carvings noting the date of his death (no religious symbol) and that he was buried with one other man.*

*The cemetery is small, lovely in every way for such a place, surrounded by a head-high red brick ornamental wall... All around are large trees (ponderosa pines, cedars, spruce, poplars)... I felt that I somehow "represented" you people because none of us has been able to pay respects to Lyndon in the past. And it is very unlikely that any of us will be able to visit there in the future. His grave is so damn remote (!) from our normal travel routes... So when I talked with Lyndon (about our younger days, the war, his death, his Nina, our parents, etc., etc.) I was talking for you, too...*

*Surely you agree that we should not feel guilt for not visiting his grave. (I certainly have not.) Nevertheless, I feel good about the trip, whatever my motives.*

*Left early Sunday, taking a different route heading north. Home in the afternoon. Phyllis had a wonderful supper (Swedish meatballs on noodles) all ready. Now everything is back to normal.*

*Yes, of course, you will get copies of the photos.*

*Love & hugs & kisses,*
*Brother Bill*

Life goes on.

**Ft. McPherson National Cemetery, Maxwell, Nebraska**

# EPILOGUE

More than fifty years have passed since I found the picture of my mother in a white wedding dress and learned that she'd once had a life I never even imagined. By that time, she had successfully buried the past for more than twenty years. But once I came running down the driveway waving that picture, she could no longer ignore her history.

Blocking out the unpleasant, the painful, and the difficult seems to have been one of Mom's fortes. So it's only natural that she would have run from the pain and grief of Lyndon's death. Within weeks of hearing the terrible news, she moved across the country and started a completely new life, with a new home, a new job, and new friends. And soon, she had a new soldier to correspond with. Within two years, she had married Dad, who effectively silenced her on the subject of her first love and marriage. And, willingly or unwillingly, she went along with it.

"Just let it go, like water off a duck's back," she'd say to my sister and me whenever we got upset. But her laissez-faire attitude could easily morph into less healthy coping mechanisms like denial, avoidance, and stuffing down whatever wasn't agreeable. There was always a price to pay eventually.

I learned at her knee. As a result, I was woefully unprepared to deal with conflict or unpleasantness once I entered the adult world. I knew that, no matter what, I was supposed to be "nice," refrain from talking back, ignore whatever I didn't like, and just get along. If (or more likely *when*) I got to the point where I just couldn't stand it, I had one option: leave. So either I submitted to the will of others or simply up and left. I developed the habit of running from job to job, man to man, and friend to friend in a panicky attempt to avoid conflict. If I just kept moving, I told myself, I wouldn't be eaten alive by everybody else. But it soon became clear that running wasn't a very satisfying way to live.

Mom reclaimed her life and sense of self when she rejoined the world as a teacher. Finding her footing in the classroom and rising to the challenges of teaching energized her. And traveling with her students broadened her world and stoked her excitement. Her power and independence grew.

But it wasn't until Dad died that the grief of losing Lyndon finally caught up with her. She'd managed to stuff it down for forty-five years, but ignoring it was no longer an option. So she hung up Lyndon's pictures, wore his rings, and sifted through her old memories. And after a while, she was free.

I found my own freedom in marriage. Not only did Barry give me love, a home, and a foundation for happiness and growth, he also helped me find a career as a writer. While writing had always come easily to me, it never occurred to me that I could become a professional writer. For one thing, I couldn't imagine what I might have to say! And yet, it happened.

It began when I edited some of Barry's projects and later wrote the occasional section or chapter. One day, he was asked to write a book about green tea but didn't have the time, so he told the editor that his wife was also a writer. I ended up getting the job, and, surprisingly, the book sold 80,000 copies. Since that time, I've made a steady living as an author. And I've found that for me the secret to success is throwing myself wholeheartedly into whatever I'm doing—whether it's writing a book, maintaining a relationship, learning to dance, planting a garden, or anything else. True satisfaction only occurs when I stop avoiding, blocking, ignoring, and running away from the impossible. The idea seems so simple and obvious, but it took a long time before I understood it.

I see now that my life and my mother's ran along parallel tracks. Both of us spent so much time denying reality that, for years, forging ahead was impossible. Yet once she faced Lyndon's death, Dad's alcoholism, and the stultifying trap of domestic life, she discovered a wealth of opportunities to grow, change, and explore. And suddenly, she learned to fly.

Later on, so did I.

## Acknowledgments

Heartfelt thanks to Dixie Matijasevich, who provided me with Lyndon's wartime letters and his Army personnel file. The book simply could not have been written without this vital information. I'm also deeply grateful to Carol Starr Schneider, an excellent writer and spot-on advisor who generously gave me her time, comments, inspiration, and encouragement throughout the many drafts of this book. Others whose enthusiasm, reassurance, and support helped immeasurably include Vera Ogren, Melinda Lewandowski, and Denise Dudley. Thanks to all of you for being there when I needed you the most!

Finally, as always, thanks to Barry Fox, my husband, teacher, true love, and live-in muse. Everything good in this world begins with you, baby—of that I'm absolutely sure.

# ABOUT THE AUTHOR

**Nadine Taylor** is the author, editor, and ghostwriter of more than twenty books in the genres of memoir, health, and business, including *New York Times* bestsellers and national bestsellers.

After twenty years as an author, she has finally written her own memoir/biography, a powerful World War II story of love, loss, and redemption as seen by a daughter searching for the truth about her mother's hidden past.

**Audiobook (narrated by Nadine) now available at:**
https://adbl.co/2KSLpnX

Book reviews posted on Amazon.com *do* make a difference and are a major factor in the success of indie authors like Nadine and indie books like *If My Heart Had Wings*.

Nadine offers sincere thanks to anyone who posts an honest review of the book at:
**www.amazon.com/If-My-Heart-Had-Wings/dp/0692057803**

Made in the USA
Monee, IL
20 June 2021

71821705R00152